MW00581775

CHICAGO WHITE SOX
1959 and Beyond

CHICAGO WHITE SOX
1959 and Beyond

Dan Helpingstine

ARCADIA
PUBLISHING

Copyright © 2004 by Dan Helpingstine
ISBN 978-1-5316-1865-0

Published by Arcadia Publishing
Charleston, South Carolina

Library of Congress Catalog Card Number: 2004107274

For all general information contact Arcadia Publishing at:
Telephone 843-853-2070
Fax 843-853-0044
E-mail sales@arcadiapublishing.com
For customer service and orders:
Toll-Free 1-888-313-2665

Visit us on the Internet at www.arcadiapublishing.com

This book is dedicated to:
Leo Bauby
Mark Liptak
Gerry Bilek
Mark Fletcher
White Sox fans and historians, one and all

CONTENTS

Two individuals who are blind take in a night game at Old Comiskey Park, 1967. Maureen Comiskey is totally blind but still is able to appreciate a good baseball game. "Sitting in the stands at a ball game is much more exciting than just listening to play-by-play on the radio," according to Comiskey. "To be a part of the crowd cheering, eating food, and the feeling the warm air is more than I could ever dream of. There is nothing like the sound of the bat cracking a baseball." Charles Comiskey, the first owner of the White Sox, is Maureen's great uncle. (Courtesy of the Gerry Bilek Photo Collection.)

INTRODUCTION

This book is a small compilation of some of the great Chicago White Sox moments from the past 45 years. It is by no means an exhaustive or all-inclusive list of games fans would like to remember. It is simply written to help fans recall some of the most memorable moments the franchise has enjoyed, laughed about or mourned over, beginning with the Sox last World Series appearance in 1959. While the White Sox are short on World Series appearances, the team has not been short on colorful teams, players and fans. Great moments should not be forgotten. They should forever be remembered no matter how sad, how maddening or how exhilarating. The White Sox have provided powerful moments that fit all three of those categories (especially the first two). This book is for the reader to enjoy even if the memories make him or her want to reach for a drink or get that prescription refilled.

It has often been said that no book is written in a vacuum. This one is no exception. I would like to thank and acknowledge the following people for helping with the production and writing of this book. Their listed order is not significant, only their contributions.

I feel a great debt to Leo Bauby, Mark Fletcher and Gerry Bilek whose contributions to this book are enormous. The pictures in this book are courtesy of their collections. They are not mere collectors, but White Sox fans who understand the significance of these photographs. By assembling these pictures, they are protecting and preserving history. More photos can be accessed at Bauby's website at www.chicago-baseball-photos.com. Leo also provided other invaluable technical assistance for preparing this book. Gerry Bilek, in addition to his collections of great photos, has an array of White Sox memorabilia that stirs memories and captures history. Mark Fletcher is a photographer as well as a collector, and his own work adds to the storytelling of the Chicago White Sox.

Mark Liptak identifies himself, wife and pets as the only White Sox fans in Chubbuck, Idaho. Having worked in the sports media for over 20 years, Liptak chronicles White Sox history with great detail. His interviews with past Sox players, posted on www.whitesoxinteractive. com, are enjoyed by Sox fans fascinated with team lore. His memories and input helped me tremendously in writing this book.

George Bova, the founder of www.whitesoxinteractive.com, turned a four-page website into a vast source of information and opinion—a great Internet place for Sox fans to visit. George provided me with information about publishing this book, for which I am grateful.

Fans who were whitesox interactive website visitors contributed to this book with their suggestions and eyewitness accounts. They added a human quality to the book, as I don't have the ability or time to go to or see every White Sox game. Their impassioned recollections put life into past events that should be remembered. And, many times, fans can act as great historians.

I am grateful to the players who allowed me time to interview them and for providing unique source material for this book. They include Donn Pall, Bill Melton, Ozzie Guillen, Joel Horlen,

Eric Soderholm, LaMarr Hoyt, Britt Burns, Jose Valentin, Jack McDowell, Jim Landis, Pete Ward and front office and long time baseball man Roland Hemond. Each, in his own way, is a large part of White Sox history.

Thanks also go to Scott Reifert of the Chicago White Sox for assisting me in obtaining the interviews of LaMarr Hoyt, Britt Burns and Jose Valentin at SoxFest 2004.

Although I was only six when the White Sox played in their last World Series, I experienced the series through two excellent books: '59 Summer of the Sox, The Year the World Series Came to Chicago by Bob Vanderberg, and Strength Down the Middle, The Story of the 1959 Chicago White Sox by Larry Kalas. Also, there is no better source of information on the Sox than The White Sox Encyclopedia written by Richard Lindberg with photo history by Mark Fletcher. Lindberg's book is one great achievement. Finally, in Crash: The Life and Times of Dick Allen, Tim Whittaker cared enough to try to explain the contradictions of a complicated man.

I am happy to include a photo taken by James A. Rasmussen of the White Sox scoreboard at the end of last night game at Old Comiskey Park. The photo captures a great moment. His website can be accessed at www.razfoto.com.

I would like to express my appreciation for Jeff Ruetsche, my editor at Arcardia. Jeff gave me the opportunity and creative freedom to put this book together.

I would be remiss if I didn't thank Nelson Freve for his technical assistance on this book. His only fault is that he is a Cub fan.

Also, I would like to thank Matt Cianchetti, a devoted Sox fan who provided me with a great story and some video highlights.

Last but not least, I owe a great amount of thanks to my wife Delia and daughter Leah, both of whom saw less of me as I worked on the book. Their support means a great deal to me.

Sportswriters on TV, from left to right, Bill Gleason, Ben Bentley, Rick Telander and Bill Jauss, discuss the White Sox prospects. Bentley is holding up a note that says, "Do Not Open Til World Series." Chicago fans are still waiting. (Courtesy of Bill Gleason.)

ONE

Pennant and Division Clinchers

This chapter unfortunately includes only three memorable moments. And choosing them required none of the selection that proved so difficult a process for the chapters that follow. Still, what happened in '59 and '83 and '93 were great moments nonetheless, even if they ended in heartbreak. The White Sox most recent claim to a World Series Championship dates back to 1917, the second longest drought in all the major leagues—and in Chicago, too. If only more memories could be recalled under the heading of "World Series Winners" . . . perhaps, someday, in a second volume.

1959—*Exorcising Demons*
Four full decades had passed.

It was in the middle of the cold war. With memories of World War II still very fresh, the United States now faced a post-war adversary that was just as formidable and scary as Adolph Hitler. Nikita Khrushchev, the leader of the Soviet Union, was in the United States, his presence making everyone nervous. Then the air raid sirens went off in Chicago, and many thought it was time to head to their fallout shelters or stick their heads between their knees.

Fortunately, the world had not ended with the beginning stages of a Russian nuclear assault. What had happened? Unbelievable as it may sound, the Chicago White Sox won the American League pennant.

"Aparicio steps on second, throws to first. Double play. Game over."

That simple description and play sequence is known by many White Sox fans, even those too young to remember or understand what happened on September 22, 1959. The Sox were playing their closest pursuers, the Cleveland Indians, in front of a crowd of 54,293 in Cleveland. A win would clinch the American League flag.

It had been such a long time—in so many ways. The White Sox had last gone to a World Series in 1919, and that Series was tainted with a scandal of the worst kind. Just who was innocent or guilty of throwing the 1919 Fall Classic to the Cincinnati Reds really didn't matter. Major League Baseball had to fight for survival, and the fall of the White Sox was a long and hard one. From 1921 to 1958, the White Sox never finished closer than five games off any pennant winner. The first years were truly rough. In 1932, the team truly bottomed out with a .325 winning percentage (.325 is a great batting average, but no every day player on the team hit .325 that year, not even the great Luke Appling) and a whopping $56^1/_2$ games behind the usual pennant winning Yankees. Amazingly the Boston Red Sox, losers of 111, dropped more games that year to save the other Sox from a last place finish.

The year 1959 would be different.

"We pretty much thought we had it," 1959 pitcher Bob Shaw told writer Bob Vanderberg, recalling the fateful game against the Indians. "But in sports you don't take anything for granted. You know it's 'Let's win the damn thing and get it over with.'" Shaw was 18-6 that year with a league leading .750 winning percentage.

During the '50s, as with so many teams in its history, the White Sox were predicated on defense and pitching. The '59 team hit only 97 homers with just two players breaking into double figures. But in that historic September game at Municipal Stadium, Al Smith and Jim Rivera hit back-to-back homers in the sixth inning to give the Pale Hose a 4-1 lead. In the ninth, the Sox led 4-2.

Wrapping it all up didn't come easily. In this case, the nail biting made the victory all the sweeter. To make Sox fans nervous, the Indians loaded the bases with one out. Reliever Gerry Staley was on the mound facing tough left handed hitting Vic Power. Power made things simpler for the Sox when he hit a grounder in the direction of the sure-fielding Luis Aparicio, greatest of all Sox shortstops.

Jim Landis was in center field and had a bird's eye view of the White Sox putting an end to 40 years of frustration. He was charging in when the ball was hit, but had a good feeling it wasn't going to get to him. "It was a rare thing when a ball got through," he recalls, referring to the fielding prowess of the Sox double play combination of Aparicio and second baseman Nelson Fox. "They were two of the best."

Landis felt two strong emotions about the pennant clinching. One was an emotional let down. After suffering a deep thigh bruise when diving back into first on a pick-off attempt, Landis finally got some action after an eight-day rest, but that was only as a ninth inning substitution. He sat glumly in the locker room feeling he had not contributed anything significant to the pennant-clinching win. First baseman Earl Torgeson came over to cheer him up, a gesture for which Landis remains grateful.

Any let down didn't last. Along with the air raid sirens, throngs of fans greeted the Sox at Midway Airport. An estimated $20,000 of damage was done to Midway, mostly to fences, as swarms of fans came to greet the new American League champions. Sharing a cab on the way home from the airport, Billy Pierce and Torgeson saw flares on the lawns of homes on Garfield Avenue, and people sitting outside in the early hours of the morning.

So it was no time for any feelings of let down. Today Landis still has his strong, happy emotions about 1959 and the team comradie of that season's ball club. "When we would go out to eat, nine guys would go," Landis remembers. "I pray the White Sox win another pennant."

Many of their fans are still praying.

The Frustration Ends

It was a long time coming.

The wait even seemed longer than 24 years, partly because the White Sox stopped contending for most seasons after a 1967 flop. Even their good teams of 1972 and 1977 were not as close as they seemed. They had good, entertaining teams those years, but any knowledgeable fan knew they were over-matched by the much stronger clubs that eventually won the division. The only thing Chicago ball clubs contended for in the '70s and the early '80s, it seemed, was the fastest exit from playoff contention.

On September 17, 1983, that changed as the Sox faced the Seattle Mariners. Fans finally experienced what they had thought was reserved only for other teams in other cities.

"Winning Ugly" had become the rallying cry of the White Sox in 1983. Texas Manager Doug Radar mistakenly decided to quote a scouting report describing White Sox victories as being "not so pretty." The White Sox and their fans were not amused. If the team wasn't inspired for any reason, it now had some inspiration—or at least a rallying cry.

Not that the Sox really needed it. They had basically steamrolled their division with rooftop homers and a starting rotation that plainly dominated hitters. No one in the West really had any thoughts about catching the Sox as the season rolled into August and September. Even during a TV interview when the Royals visited Chicago in late August, future Hall of Famer George Brett nearly conceded the title to the Sox.

But Chicago fans, naturally, wanted the title wrapped up as soon as possible. Nightmares of 1967 were still too vivid for many, and in Chicago, baseball success is never taken for granted.

Rain delayed the beginning of the Mariners game, which was sort of typical of Chicago White Sox luck. An owners' lockout of the players had canceled a big crowd for the season opener in 1972, and snow wiped out another potential stadium-packed opener ten years later. Why shouldn't this gratification be delayed as well?

"There was no way they weren't going to play that game," says Bob James, baseball guru and Sox fan. James sat down the first base line in the second to the last row of the upper deck. "The crowd was absolutely riveted during the whole game. Time went by so fast, it seemed like five minutes."

By the eighth inning, it looked like things were well in hand. Harold Baines hit his third homer in three days, and the Sox had a 3-1 lead. It wasn't a rout, but, with White Sox pitching, a two run lead in the ninth seemed more than safe.

But the Mariners, a team that still didn't have a winning record since their inception in 1977, were not going to let the Sox off that easily. Rickey Nelson doubled in Al Cowens and Harold Reynolds to earn the Mariners a 3-3 tie.

In a way, this was better. The Sox came to bat in the bottom of the ninth in full control of their own destiny. And the ninth provided a memory that will forever stay with all Sox fans of that era.

In an indirect manner, the Sox received some help from the Cubs. Ex-Cub reliever Bill Caudill walked three straight Sox hitters after getting Jerry Hairston to line out. The third hitter, Carlton Fisk was awarded first on a disputed call; the Mariners contending that he went around for a strike. Even Sox fan James thought Fisk was going to be called out. But the umpires wouldn't be swayed by Seattle's protest. It was a break for the Sox, and an indication of the kind of season it had turned out to be, at least up to that point.

Baines stepped up to the plate, and that was appropriate. In the early '80s Major League Baseball had a statistic called the Game Winning RBI (GWRBI), and Baines, with 21, was one of the league leaders. And though it was considered a misleading stat—often the GWRBI was not the actual game winner—there wasn't anything misleading about Baines as a clutch hitter. As his eighth-inning home run that night had shown, Baines was in the habit of coming through with the key late inning hit.

Baines didn't deliver a hit this time, but he did what he had to do. He sent a fly to center that was more than deep enough to bring in Julio Cruz from third. The Western Division Title, for the first time, now belonged to the Chicago White Sox.

"We went crazy after Cruz scored," James said. "People were high fiving everybody. We had the unbelievable feeling that it was actually happening. We went on the field. I didn't see a single fight or any rough stuff. It was the just pure joy of a celebration."

Henry Ortiz was 15 at the time and decided that nothing was going to stop him from attending that game. He and an older friend had bought tickets in the street. Sitting in the first row of the left center field lower deck, Ortiz wasted no time in getting down to the field. "I jumped over the wall and landed in a mud puddle by the time Cruz scored," Ortiz recalls. "They couldn't stop people from going onto the field. There was no violence, no destroying things. It was electric." The young Ortiz was also elated to see his face on the centerfield scoreboard as images of the celebration were flashed for all there to see.

Another milestone was achieved that night. With the 45,646 in the stands, the 1983 Chicago White Sox became the first Chicago baseball team in history to pass the 2 million mark in attendance. This from a team that only three years earlier looked like it was on its way out of town.

Unfortunately, Chicago baseball luck returned to form as the Sox were beaten by the Baltimore Orioles in the American League Championship Series. But what transpired at Comiskey on September 17, 1983, may have changed Chicago's sports fortunes for the next ten years. During that time span, the Bears won the Super Bowl, the Bulls won three NBA championships, the Cubs won two division crowns, the Sox won another division, and the Black Hawks made a rare appearance in the Stanley Cup Finals. And it all started with Julio Cruz raising his fist in the air after emphatically tagging home plate with the winning run that clinched a long awaited baseball championship in Chicago.

The Last Western Division Championship

Ten years had passed.

In Chicago baseball terms that is not a really long time between championships. However, once Sox had fans had experienced a first place finish, it seemed a very long decade indeed. Nineteen Eighty-Four was a disaster; the late '80s were nothing but rebuilding and losing; and, in 1990, the club didn't have much of a chance of taking its division despite winning 94 games.

The 1993 team was accused by some of being under-achievers, but one of the biggest stories of that season was an over-achieving Vincent "Bo" Jackson. Jackson was a true rarity, playing Major League Baseball and then spending his off-season as a running back for the NFL Oakland Raiders. His football career was finished and his baseball career was jeopardized by a football hip injury during a playoff game on January 13, 1991. Eventually having to live with an artificial hip, Jackson was released by the Royals in 1991, and then signed by the Sox. He had but 71 plate appearances that season. He didn't play at all in 1992.

It was a long rehab process. Working closely with team trainer Herm Schnieder, Jackson had to invest a lot of hard work and time just to get in good enough shape to take a step back on the baseball field, much less be a productive major leaguer.

Jackson was honored by the Chicago area sportswriters at their annual "Diamond Dinner" held at the Palmer House on January 23, 1993. On receiving awards at this dinner, the player made a brief speech. Jackson chose to thank Schnieder for all his help, described the man as "his date," and asked Schnieder to stand up. The shy acting Sox trainer didn't move and Jackson scowled as he looked over the crowd of over 1,000. "I said stand up!" Jackson boomed into the microphone, his deep voice resonating throughout the room. Schnieder stood up.

In 1993 Jackson hit two unforgettable home runs for the Sox, both having a whopping emotional impact. The first was hit on April 9 against the Yankees in Jackson's first at bat since rehabilitation. Sox fans gave him a standing ovation as he stepped in and hit what he thought was a routine pop-up to right field. There was nothing routine about it. His "pop-up" landed several rows up in the seats for a dramatic home run.

Gerry Bilek sat in right field and had a great view of the home run as it soared over his head, landing about four rows behind him. "A boy about thirteen had come up with the ball," Bilek said. "Dozens of fans slapped on the back, high fived him, and celebrated both the event and the treasure itself. Within a matter of seconds a couple of Sox security personnel came up to the boy and asked for the ball, saying 'Bo wants it.' The boy looked around for his father who unfortunately missed the event at the concession or restroom. The boy looked very unsure of what to do. We told him to wait for his father."

Bilek said he heard numerous interviews with the boy who eventually traded the ball for some memorabilia. The ball is bronzed and has been placed on the gravestone of Jackson's late mother, according to Bilek. Jackson had promised her, shortly before she passed away, that he would once again play baseball.

On September 27 Jackson clubbed his other big home run of the season. It would turn out to have just as powerful an emotional impact. The Sox needed one win to clinch the Western Division. As with their first crown clinching, Chicago was playing the Seattle Mariners.

With two men on in the sixth, Jackson hit again what he thought was a routine fly, this time to left. Mariner left field Brian Turang tracked the high drive in the swirling Chicago wind. When Turang found his way to the wall, it looked like he would make a leap, but the homer was too far into the seats for him even to make the attempt. Gerry Bilek was at this game also and thought the ball sort of "wafted gently over the fence . . . There seemed to be a delayed reaction before the crowd went wild," Bilcek recalls. "I think some of the crowd wasn't sure the ball made it over the fence, and others were in awe of the magnitude of the pop-up. Bo launched the highest fly ball I have ever witnessed."

In the ninth, Kirk McCaskill was on the mound for the Sox. After throwing a fastball for a strike, McCaskill threw two sweeping curves to Brett Boone. Boone struck out having never come close to hitting the ball. One out.

Next up was Dave Magadan. The big left-hitting first baseman hit a grounder that looked like a sure single to right. Craig Grebeck flagged the ball down on the outfield grass and made a beautiful off-balanced throw to McCaskill covering first. Two out.

Dave Valle was Seattle's last hope. He picked on an outside pitch and sent a harmless looking fly to right. Ellis Burks made the routine catch. Five pitches, three outs, division championship.

The ballpark, with fans waving white socks, rocked and sounded like Old Comiskey in 1977. A rebuilding process, began in the late '80s, had finally paid off.

Jackson trotted around New Comiskey after the game to celebrate the title clinching. He would not make a significant contribution in the playoffs, which the Sox lost. In 1994 he played his final game of baseball with the Angels, never quite fulfilling the promise that seemed to be all his during the late '80s.

Still, he was a great story for the White Sox, even with the team again failing to get to the World Series. His towering home run won't be remembered just because it helped clinch a division; in a cynical age of obscene amounts of money paid and generated by Major League Baseball, it is testimony to a man who overcame great adversity through his will to simply play baseball once again.

Bill Veeck shows his form on the mound during the 1959 White Sox home opener, April 14, 1959. It was the first full season when the Comiskey family didn't have controlling interest in the club. Veeck won the pennant that year, but he was later criticized for squandering other potential pennants by trading young hitters who would prove to be big stars in the '60s.

14

A truly rare picture, the Chicago White Sox celebrate on the field after winning the 1959 American League pennant. (Courtesy of the Gerry Bilek Photo Collection.)

It's September 22, 1959, and the White Sox celebrate their first pennant in 40 years in the locker room in Cleveland. Someone is about to get a beer shampoo. (Courtesy of the Gerry Bilek Photo Collection.)

Julio Cruz signals "one out" during Game Four of the 1983 American League Championship Series. Cruz went three for three that day but no one could drive him in. A big part of the Winning Ugly champions, Cruz was never the same after that year because of a turf toe injury. For ten years the Sox weren't the same, either. (Courtesy of the Leo Bauby Photo Collection.)

Julio Cruz dances across home plate for the winning run against the Seattle Mariners on September 17, 1983. It was now official. The Chicago White Sox were Western Division Champions. Time for another celebration! (Courtesy of the Leo Bauby Photo Collection.)

Now everyone joins in. Somewhere in the middle of that pile is Julio Cruz. In addition to clinching the 1983 Western Division title, the White Sox went over the 2 million mark in attendance—a Chicago baseball first. (Courtesy of the Mark Fletcher Photo Collection.)

It's September 19, 1983, and the flag declaring the Chicago White Sox Western Division Champions is raised. Doing the honors on the right center field roof is first baseman Mike Squires. (Courtesy of the Leo Bauby Photo Collection.)

Throngs of well-wishers converge in downtown Chicago in a send off to the Winning Ugly 1983 White Sox. The rally didn't help. (Courtesy of the Leo Bauby Photo Collection.)

The quiet Harold Baines follows through on a swing. Baines provided many a clutch hit for the Winning Ugly team and compiled just under 3,000 for his career. His No. 3 would be retired, though he came back as a player and a coach two decades later. (Courtesy of the Gerry Bilek Photo Collection.)

Bo Jackson is in an intense looking mood while still with Kansas City. Jackson hit the game-winning homer in the division title clinching game of 1993. He also homered in his first plate appearance since 1991 in the Sox 1993 home opener. He will be remembered for his sheer determination to make it back to baseball after football hip injury. (Courtesy of the Mark Fletcher Photo Collection.)

It was always fun watching Ozzie Guillen at the plate. A singles hitter, but yet a free swinger, Guillen took a hack at anything that was close. Shortstop for the 1993 division champions, Guillen began the 2004 season as Sox manager. (Photo by Mark Fletcher.)

TWO

Great Pitching Performances

Nothing in baseball compares to a perfect game, or no-hitter. To witness a no-hitter, or any complete game shutout for that matter, is to see a great ballgame. Often, it is history. Anytime an ace takes the mound and throws a gem, with all the skill (and luck) involved in a dominating pitching performance, it is a truly memorable moment. And the White Sox—a team so long built on the philosophy of strong pitching beating strong hitting—have provided plenty of such gems over the past 45 years.

A No-Hitter in the Middle of a Pennant Race

The wheels were falling off the wagon.

A cliché for certain, but it's the best way to describe the situation facing the Chicago White Sox on September 10, 1967. The Sox were among four teams fighting for first place in the next-to-the-last season of one-divisional baseball. Going into a doubleheader with the Detroit Tigers, Chicago was two games behind that day's front-runners, the Tigers and Minnesota, and one and a half games behind the Red Sox. With the standings at the top changing almost daily, the fourth place Sox were in great striking distance. True, two games were not much to make up with 21 left for the Sox to play. However, Chicago suddenly looked vulnerable and some thought they were no longer in the race.

Detroit had come to Chicago for a four game series. The Tigers won a Friday night game one 4-1. In game two, the Sox blew a 3-0 ninth inning lead, serving up seven runs to the Tigers in the final frame before going down meekly for a 7-3 loss. Some critics pronounced the Sox deader than dead. Manager Eddie Stanky, a throwback player (now a throwback manager), took quite an exception to the doomsday predictions. "They discount the guts of this club," Stanky said, sounding like a drill sergeant. "All year long this team has had guts."

This was not the first time Stanky felt it necessary to publicly defend his ballclub. Just two and a half weeks earlier, the testy manager stood up against the criticism that described the light hitting White Sox as "dull." This leveled criticism came at a time when the Sox were tied with the Red Sox for first place. "We're last in homers, we're last in hitting, and we're last in war and peace," an irritated Stanky said lashing out. "But we're first in guts and determination."

Stanky deserved credit for supporting his ballplayers, especially after such a tough loss. However, veteran Pete Ward thought the Sox were on the brink of destruction after the 7-3 defeat, despite the team's guts and determination. "We knew we had to do something," Ward told this author, referring the series-ending Sunday doubleheader. "Things were falling apart."

Joel Horlen, the 1967 team ace, was slated to start game three, first the doubleheader. Going into the start with a 15-6 record, the Texas born right-hander was having a breakout year. In his understated way he told the author, "I was probably more relaxed and focused in 1967."

Horlen was not a bad pitcher in the previous three seasons. He sported ERAs of 1.88, 2.88 and 2.43. Despite these impressive numbers, Horlen had not been a big winner, never gaining more than 13 wins. In an age with the best starting pitchers threw complete games or at least expected to get to the eighth or ninth, Horlen was tagged by his pitching coach as a pitcher who lost concentration in the late innings. Was this one reason why he'd only won 36 games in that three-year stretch?

His toughest defeat came on July 29, 1963. Playing in Washington when the nation's capital still had a franchise, the Sox faced the Senators. Going into the ninth inning, Horlen had a no-hitter and was trying to protect a 1-0 lead. Right fielder Jim King led off and grounded to second baseman Nelson Fox. Horlen now was only two outs away from making baseball notability. Left fielder Chuck Hinton followed with another grounder. Only this one skipped right past Horlen's feet and up the middle into center field. The no-hitter was gone. Two batters later, with two outs, power hitting Don Luck sent a deep drive over a leaping Sox left fielder Dave Nicholson, and over the fence for a two-run homer.

Joel Horlen went from making baseball history to being a 2-1 loser. The Sox pitcher looked devastated as he left the field, almost bumping into the triumphant Lock who was completing his home run trot.

Although he had lost that game in Washington, Horlen was learning the lesson about keeping his pitches down in the strike zone. In that fateful ninth inning, three of the balls were on the ground, even the single that broke up the no-hitter. "Location" was the practice that 1967 Manager Stanky also preached and pounded into his pitchers. Horlen was grateful for the lesson.

"He got you to play," Horlen said of the manager who had alienated many. "He was the only manager who ever fined me, and I still loved him."

With a past that left him wanting for more, Horlen took the mound against the Tigers that bright day, four summers after having come so close. Detroit had the likes of Al Kaline, Norm Cash and Willie Horton in its lineup. They would go on to hit a team total of 152 homers in 1967, a pretty hefty number in that day and age. Beating them on any day, much less in the middle of a tight pennant race, was more than a tough task. Fortunately for Horlen, the Sox made things a little easier by scoring five times in the first inning.

Things became more complicated when Horlen hit Tiger catcher Bill Freehan with a pitch in the third. It was the third day in a row that the big catcher had been hit. Horlen insisted that none of it was intentional. "He stood on top of the plate," Horlen said, "but we still had to throw inside."

Neither Freehan nor the Tigers were very understanding. Since there was no designated hitter in 1967, American League pitchers hit for themselves. Horlen came up in the fourth and tried to have a brief conversation with Freehan, hoping bygones would be bygones. But Freehan wasn't talking. Tiger pitcher Dave Wickersham kept throwing at Horlen until he hit the Sox pitcher on the inside of the knee. Horlen was hurt badly enough that he couldn't sit for the rest of the game, pacing the dugout between innings.

Horlen's injury may have stopped him from taking a seat, but it didn't stop him from dominating the Tigers. In the fourth, Al Kaline hit a soft liner that appeared to be heading into shallow right for a single, but was caught by second baseman Wayne Causey who timed his leap perfectly. Eddie Mathews hit a deep fly that was flagged down by right fielder Bill Voss in the eighth. Other than those two drives, the Tigers didn't come close to getting a hit. After the Sox picked up one more in their half of the eighth, Joel Horlen again stood on the verge of a no-hitter.

Before the inning began, catcher J C Martin went out to talk to Horlen. When Martin asked Horlen what he wanted to do, the Sox pitcher told Martin he had gotten him this far, and he should take him the rest of the way.

Infielder Jerry Lumpe led off with a grounder that seemed destined for right center field. Sox second baseman Wayne Causey ranged far to his right and backhanded the ball. Causey had run so far he was now totally off balance and had a tough throw. Literally holding himself up on one foot, Causey threw a lollypop while falling backwards, and ball floated to first baseman

Cotton Nash. As Nash stretched, the ball and runner seemed to get to first at the same time. The umpire's call was emphatic. Lumpe was out.

Lumpe and Tiger Manager Mayo Smith had a simultaneous fit. While they screamed at the first base ump, WGN-TV ran a replay. It appeared the Lumpe was indeed safe, but replays don't count and this time Horlen got the benefit of a close call. One down.

Catcher Phil Heath was next. He grounded out to third baseman Don Buford on a more routine play. One to go.

Dick McAuliffe was next, a shortstop with power and not an easy last out for Horlen. McAuliffe sent a grounder to shortstop Ron Hansen that seemed to hop 50 times. Hansen fielded the ball cleanly and then took his time to ensure a good grip. Jack Brickhouse, doing one of his last Sox TV play-by-plays, was getting antsy in the booth. "Throw it, Ron, throw it," Brickhouse yelled. Ron threw it. McAuliffe was out. The no-hitter was complete.

Pete Ward had said the Sox needed to do something. Well, Horlen did. By staying to a pitching game plan that stressed location rather than mere pitch speed, Horlen picked up 20 outs as a result of the groundball. The wheels were back on the wagon.

The Sox won the second game of the doubleheader 4-0. Four days later they beat the Cleveland Indians 1-0 in 17 innings. In that game lefty Gary Peters gave up one hit in the second inning but no more during an 11-inning stint. The next day Chicago shut out Cleveland again, this time 4-0 in ten innings. In the space of five days, the Sox pitching staff threw an equivalent of five shutouts allowing only 14 hits in 45 innings. They were back in the pennant race.

Unfortunately for the Sox, their much-criticized lack of hitting cost them a chance at the World Series. But the Horlen no-hitter was a truly remarkable White Sox pitching performance. Horlen, no longer the hard luck pitcher, had given his team a real chance by coming through with the clutch performance of his career.

A Great Starting Pitcher . . . for A Reliever
He was a bright spot in an almost historic season.

Wilbur Wood appeared in 184 games from 1971 to 1974, starting almost every one. He won 90 in that four-year stretch and had 84 complete games. Yet Wood, who worked as a reliever in the early part on his career, wanted to remain in that role. He appeared in 88 games in 1968, all out of the bullpen, and won 13, which made him the winningest pitcher on the Sox staff that miserable year. So when he was approached to become a starter for the pitching-thin Sox in 1971, Wood wasn't warm to the idea.

"Wilbur wasn't too keen about it in the beginning," former Sox GM Roland Hemond recalls. "He saw himself as a successful relief pitcher. He thought he found his niche . . . He made our staff better because of the innings he pitched. He would go the distance and the bullpen rested on the days he pitched. And they [the bullpen] could pick up pitchers on other days because they weren't being used so often."

There was no better example of this than his effort against the Oakland A's on August 12, 1972. The White Sox were the only true competition the A's had for the Western Division crown that season. Playing in Oakland, the Sox were in second place, one game behind the A's.

Wood was on the mound facing John "Blue Moon" Odom. Neither team could generate an offense. In fact, Wood had a no-hitter until the seventh when he gave up a two out single to right fielder Brant Alyea. Chicago finally broke through in the ninth. Dick Allen tripled and came home on a sacrifice fly by Carlos May. With Wood on the mound, it appeared that one run was all the Sox needed to pull out a win. With two out in the bottom of the ninth, Brant Alyea struck again. He homered to tie the game, still the only Oakland player to have a hit. Wood had pitched a complete two-hit, one-run game to that point, but had nothing but a no-decision to show for his considerable efforts.

In early July, the pennant hopes of the Sox had suffered a major setback when it was announced that third baseman Bill Melton was out for the rest of the year due to a bad back. GM Hemond made a quick trade and picked up third baseman Ed Spiezio. It turned out that

Spiezio was in almost as bad a shape as Melton. According to Hemond, Spiezio played the remainder of the '72 season with a broken rib. No one in the front office or field management knew about the injury. Hemond said he found out about the condition when he visited Spiezio some 25 years later.

Spiezio was not the offensive threat Melton had been in 1970 and 1971. He was an excellent defensive player who gave the team some stability at third. In this game, he did more than give defensive support. He delivered just one of many big hits the Sox came up with that year. In the top of the 11th inning, he knocked a two-run homer to left to give the Sox a 3-1 lead. Rollie Fingers, one of the best relievers of that day, gave up the gopher ball.

Wood was still in the game and came out for the 11th. Showing no signs of tiring, the knuckleball throwing Wood retired the hard hitting A's in order, not allowing the ball out of the infield. The pitcher, who had been hesitant to come out of the bullpen, won his 20th game, breaking the 20 win barrier for the second straight season.

Wood finished the game surrendering just those two hits to Alyea. Bert Camperneris, Joe Rudi, Sal Bando, Gene Tenace, Dave Duncan, Tim Cullen, and some guy named Mangual all went hitless. The A's went three up and three down six times and only seriously threatened on one occasion. The win pushed the Sox into a virtual tie for first with the West Coast ball club.

The win was so typical for Wood. Given the minimum of support, he made a small lead stand up. And at that point, it appeared that he would win the American League Cy Young Award. He would shut out Oakland the next month, but, unfortunately, Wood went into a late season slump and then lost his last decision 1-0, depriving him of a 25th victory. The award instead went to Gaylord Perry, the guy who liked to put saliva on the ball.

No Sox pitcher since has come close to matching Wilbur Wood's accomplishments in the early '70s, a time when the left-hander often took the mound on only two days rest. Try to picture the Sox contending for anything in 1972 without Wood as their number one starter. You can't. Not bad for a relief pitcher.

Near Perfection
Twenty-seven up, 27 down.

That is what they call a perfect game in baseball, a truly a rare and historic occasion. On May 2, 1984, it almost happened at Old Comiskey Park. LaMarr Hoyt, fresh off a Cy Young Award winning season for a division winning team, shut down the New York Yankees in dominating style. He gave up but one hit—a wind blown blooper between shortstop Jerry Dybzinski and left fielder Ron Kittle. The only Yankee base runner was Don Mattingly, who was erased on a double play. The Yankees sent the minimum 27 batters to the plate.

"For the rest of my life, I will consider that a perfect game," Hoyt recalls.

Hoyt was in a tough frame of mind that night. He was off to a poor start in '84, sporting only a 2-2 mark going into the contest. And he had incentive to prove something to the Yankee organization. New York had traded him to the Sox on April 5, 1977, in the deal that sent Bucky Dent to the Yankees in exchange for Oscar Gamble. His pride still hurting, he always wanted to pitch well against them.

The combination of his seven-year-old hard feelings towards the Yankees and disappointment for his slow start didn't put Hoyt in the best of the moods as he took the mound that night. "I already had steam coming out of my ears before I went to the mound," Hoyt recalls.

However, bad karma wasn't all he had going that night. He says that everything was working for him from a pitching standpoint. "A lot of times you're basically dealing with eighty percent of your capacity," he says. "Other words, it is very seldom you are going to walk out with one hundred percent of what you expect. So you have to learn to pitch with the rest of your repertoire. When you got it all together in a single night, in a single moment, and you know it, and I knew it, it didn't discourage me at all when they got that hit."

For the first $6^1/_3$ innings, everything was there. In one inning after another, the Yankees didn't come close to getting a hit. Only four balls left the infield. There were no real close calls, nothing threatened to drop in or sneak through the infield. With the exception of when Willie Randolph led off the game with a grounder that Hoyt deflected to shortstop Dybzinksi, the Yankees went three up, three down rather quietly.

The seventh began the same way when Willie Randolph struck out. Hoyt was eight outs away from a no-hitter, if not perfection, when Don Mattingly stepped to the plate. The final box score shows that Mattingly picked up a single in that at-bat. Knowing Mattingly, fans would probably think it was some kind of line shot. Nothing could be further from the truth.

As soon as the ball left the bat, it looked like trouble, not because it was hit hard, but because it was a pop up without a lot of altitude, capable of plopping down safely anywhere. The gusty wind didn't help matters either, making it hard for any fielder to judge the ball quickly. To add to everything else, Kittle did not have a terrific jump, and Dybzinski had to run out with his back to the infield, not an easy play for him. There was a fear of the two fielders colliding.

Soon it was obvious no one was in position to make any kind of play. Dybzinksi dove out of desperation. He couldn't even tip the ball with his outstretched glove. With the hard bounce, the ball bounded right up to Kittle. The no-hitter and the perfect game were gone in one moment. While Hoyt had everything going for him pitching-wise, he ran out of the luck that often is needed for a no-hit game.

Many times a pitcher becomes a little unnerved when he loses a no-hitter late in the game. Other than feeling a little disappointed over losing a shot at history, was Hoyt shook up any? Additionally, the Sox lead was only 3-0, and the game's outcome was still in doubt.

"I didn't care," Hoyt says. "I was used to winning a lot of games but we weren't playing up to what we should have been playing. I was the number one starter, and I felt it was up to me to shut the door, slam the door, start a winning streak—whatever. I was going to do it that night, and nothing was going to stop me."

The next hitter was left fielder Steve Kemp. Hoyt was familiar with Kemp since the outfielder had spent the 1982 season with the Sox. Hoyt also knew that shortstop Dybzinksi was cheating toward second for the fastball-hitting outfielder. Kemp bounced one right back to the mound. Hoyt may not have lost concentration after losing his no-hit bid, but he seemed to be angry at the world when he turned and fired a laser beam toward second.

"I just threw a bullet right over second," Hoyt recalls. "I knew he [Dybzinski] was there or was going to be there."

Cheating toward second, Dybzinksi took the throw, forced out Mattingly, and his relay easily nailed Kemp for a double play. The Yankees got a hit, but through eight innings they had only sent up the minimum number of batters.

In the Yankee ninth, Ken Griffey Sr. grounded out to second baseman Scott Fletcher. One down. Rick Cerone looked like he was going to pick up the Yankees' second hit when he sent a line shot to center, but Rudy Law made a diving catch just before the ball could hit the ground. Two down. Butch Wynegar struck out to end the game.

"When I walked off the mound, I started thinking about how I only faced twenty-seven batters," Hoyt says. "I didn't care if they did get a hit." Twenty years later, Hoyt has not changed his mind and still looks at this as a perfect game. Remembering Mattingly's Texas leaguer, one would have a hard time arguing with him.

History Made by a Future Hall of Famer
Three hundred wins are no joking matter.

He came to the Mets when the Mets were the running joke of Major League Baseball. Playing in a new stadium that was right smack-dab in the middle of a major airport flight pattern, the New York Metropolitans were associated with losing and comical play. Their first few losing seasons have been chronicled for their amusement, not in memory of winning streaks or heroic moments.

Tom Seaver began his career with the Mets in 1967 when the Mets were still very bad. Seaver made a triumphant appearance in the classic 1967 All-Star Game, which the National League won 2-1 in 15 innings. He preserved the win for the Senior Circuit by pitching the last inning, striking out White Sox center fielder Ken Berry to end the game with a curve that no one could have hit. Seaver won the National League Rookie of the Year Award that season. On NBC's Tonight Show, Johnny Carson had an actor playing the role of Seaver. Carson presented the "award" to the actor, which the man promptly dropped. The "award" shattered, and the audience was stunned that the young man's prestigious award was in pieces on the floor. Carson later explained that the young man was an actor and not Seaver, and that the whole thing was a joke.

But Seaver's career was no joke. Seaver gained his Rookie of the Year Honors by winning 16 games for a last place team that lost 101. He won the National League's Cy Young Award in 1969, '73 and '75. He led the National League with the lowest ERA on three occasions and won 20 games or more five times. On April 22, 1970, Seaver set a record for consecutive strikeouts in a game during a 2-1 Mets win over the San Diego Padres. Ten straight Padres whiffed in that contest.

After winning the 1983 Western Division, the White Sox felt they could part company with reliever Dennis Lamp, losing Lamp to free agency. They were able to pluck a player from the player compensation pool as a result. The Sox picked Seaver.

With a dominant looking starting staff of LaMarr Hoyt, Richard Dotson and Floyd Bannister, Sox fans salivated at the idea of Seaver joining the club. Seaver did have a good year in 1984 when he led the staff with 15 wins. Ironically, he probably could have won 20, but the relief staff, missing the departed Lamp, couldn't hold some of Seaver's leads. Regardless, Seaver was poised for more history making in 1985. He needed only 12 wins to reach the coveted 300-win milestone.

On July 19, Seaver picked up win number 298. Facing the Cleveland Indians, he led 1-0 with the tying run on second and two outs in the ninth. Manager Tony LaRussa came out for a conference and was joined on the mound by catcher Carlton Fisk. Seaver hinted that he might like to be relieved for the last out of the game. Fisk, who represented the only run of the game, hitting his 24th home run in the second, informed Seaver that he was staying in the game. Fisk reminded Seaver that he didn't get to that point in his career by letting other pitchers finish his work for him. Seaver meekly responded to this admonishment by saying, "Yes, sir." Seaver then induced Julio Franco to hit a harmless fly to center fielder Reid Nichols to end the contest.

On August 4, 1985, Seaver returned to New York in his first attempt to win 300. The Sox played the Yankees in front of a crowd of over 54,000. New York still loved Seaver, but the city now preferred he make his history elsewhere.

The White Sox scored four in the sixth and took a 4-1 lead into the last inning. Seaver was still on the mound, not wanting a reliever to come in this time.

The ninth inning was a rough one. Dan Pasqua began by singling. Seaver got a little breathing room by striking out Yankee catcher Ron Hassey. Seaver's heart must have jumped when he saw Willie Randolph's drive to right; Harold Baines made the catch for the Sox, but had to drape himself all over the right field wall to do it. He just needed one more out, but he walked Mike Pagliarulo to bring the tying run to the plate. Don Baylor, a future Cub manager, came in to pinch hit for Bobby Meacham. Baylor, a power-hitting outfielder, was a definite threat to tie the game with a long ball.

The confrontation didn't last long. Seaver threw an off speed pitch to Baylor. The result was a routine fly ball, again to Reid Nichols, who was now in left. Nichols secured the ball with both hands, and "Tom Terrific" had his 300th win.

The Hitless Wonders
What pitcher would want to forget his own no-hitter?

The Hitless Wonders tag has been hung around the White Sox since 1906 and has never seemed to go away. In the year 1906, the White Sox appeared in their first World Series and beat a Cub team that won 116 regular season games. The Sox hit a grand total of seven homers during their regular season before besting the Cubs in six games. In 1959, they hit many more, ending up with 97, not an overly impressive amount even in those days. In 1967, the Sox hit a measly .225 as a team and came within three games of a World Series.

On July 1, 1990, the White Sox truly gave a new meaning to the term "Hitless Wonders." They were no-hit and they won.

It was only the 13th time that a pitcher or combination of pitchers had thrown a no-hitter and lost, and the first time it had occurred since 1967 when Baltimore's Steve Barber and Stu Miller combined for a no-hitter only to lose to Detroit 2-1.

"I'm stunned," said Yankee pitcher Andy Hawkins. "This is not the way I envisioned a no-hitter. I always dreamed of getting the last out and then jumping up and down."

The only players who jumped up and down were wearing White Sox uniforms. Nineteen Ninety was a strange year with a team of over achievers continuing to win. In this game they didn't give the appearance of scoring any runs or getting any hits. Only the strong effort of left-handed starter Greg Hibbard kept them in the game. Hibbard pitched seven innings, gave up four harmless singles and walked no one. But even he didn't get credit for the win.

By the eighth inning, it didn't look like either team wanted to win the game. The Sox first two hitters went out as both catcher Ron Karkovice and second baseman Scott Fletcher popped out in the infield. Then Sammy Sosa stepped up.

This wasn't the same Sammy Sosa who later crashed the 60-homer barrier. Still practically a rookie, Sosa hit 15 homers 1990. In the eighth inning of this game, his grounder to third baseman Mike Blowers was bobbled, and Sosa beat the throw to first with a headfirst slide. Sox Manager Jeff Torborg felt that Sosa's speed influenced Blowers in hurrying and then misplaying the grounder.

Hawkins then made trouble for himself by walking Ozzie Guillen and Lance Johnson to load the bases. What followed was a comedy of errors that was not at all funny to Hawkins or the Yankees.

Robin Ventura lifted a fly to left that normally would have ended the inning. But outfielder Jim Leyritz battled the wind and lost. He dropped the fly, and with two outs and everybody running, three runs scored.

Ivan Calderon was next and he hit another normally routine fly to right. Jesse Barfield lost the ball in the sun and let it go off his glove for another error. Ventura scored to make it 4-0. So, in the inning, there were three errors, two walks, no hits and four runs. Even the 1906 Sox would have had a hard time competing with those results.

The winning pitcher in the game? Barry Jones, who faced three batters in the eighth, barely working up a sweat. A "stunned" Andy Hawkins got the no-hitter, and the loss.

Debut no-hitter

Just who is this Wilson Alvarez guy?

This is a question White Sox fans had to be asking themselves on August 11, 1991. In the midst of the tight division race with the Minnesota Twins, the Sox sent out Alvarez to start a Sunday afternoon contest against the Baltimore Orioles. Many times contending teams like to go out and trade for a veteran pitcher to help stabilize a staff late in the season. Instead, the Sox called up the young Alvarez who had never been in a major league pennant race in his life.

On July 24, 1989, Alvarez had his first start in the major leagues when with the Texas Rangers. It was not the greatest of debuts. The young lefty gave up a single, a homer, another homer, a walk and then another walk. He took the loss in a 6-3 Texas defeat.

Five days later, Alvarez was traded with Sammy Sosa and infielder Scott Fletcher for Harold Baines and infielder Fred Manrique. The White Sox were in the middle of a rebuilding stage. No one had heard of any of the Ranger players except for Fletcher, who had been on the 1983 White Sox division winning team. Alvarez was sent to a minor league assignment, and fans quickly forgot him. He didn't make a major league appearance for the Sox until his starting assignment against Baltimore.

So what does the rookie do in his first start for the White Sox and only second major league appearance? He throws a no-hitter.

Since he got no one out in his first start in 1989, his career ERA was infinite. Alvarez got off to a much better start in this game. He struck out the side and actually led 2-0 because of a two-run Frank Thomas blast in the top of the first.

Except for a throwing error by catcher Ron Karkovice in the seventh and three walks, the Orioles couldn't put on any runners as the game headed into the ninth. Meanwhile, on the strength of 14 hits, the White Sox had built a 7-0 lead. Going into the ninth, the only suspense was whether or not the rookie was going to get his no-hitter.

Everything went according to script with the first two batters. Mike Devereaux flied out to Lance Johnson, and some guy named Bell struck out. Then Alvarez made Sox fans nervous by walking Cal Ripken and Darrell Evans. But then he struck out Randy Milligan to end the game and preserve his place in baseball and White Sox history.

The reaction by the Sox faithful was somewhat Cub-fan like. Some predicted a Cy Young Award for Alvarez, a highly unlikely event for someone beginning his season in August. Others now felt safe enough to dream of a World Series for the Sox. With the dramatic Alvarez win, they were in second place, one game behind Minnesota.

Needless to say, the American League Cy Young Award went to someone else that year. As for the Sox as a team, their fortunes did not include a World Series. They lost 13 out of their next 15, and were no-hit themselves by Royals right-hander Brett Saberhagen. By September 1, they had lost $7^1/_2$ games in the standings to the Twins since the Alvarez no-hitter, and it was now safe to say the season was over.

Alvarez would fulfill some of his promise during the next few years, winning 15 games in 1993 and another 15 in 1996. He was the winning pitcher in the title clincher in 1993, his seventh straight win, and his complete game effort in the playoffs against Toronto helped keep the Sox alive in that series. In 1997, he was one of the players involved in the controversial "White Flag Trade" when he was traded with pitchers Roberto Hernandez and Danny Darwin in exchange for six unknowns.

Success was fleeting for Alvarez after leaving the Sox, though had somewhat of a comeback 2003 when he won six late season games for the Dodgers. Yet on August 11, 1991, he was the talk of the Chicago sports town. Big things were predicted for him for that year and beyond. On that day, 21-year-old Wilson Alvarez had made only his second major league appearance. His no-hitter remains (through 2003) the last one thrown by a Sox pitcher.

A Masterpiece

The ten-hitter can be a pitching gem, too.

Minnesota Twins pitcher Jim Deshaies pitched his heart out against the White Sox on August 22, 1993, in the Metrodome. The left-hander logged in eight innings, gave up three hits, one run and walked no one. After giving up a solo home run to Frank Thomas in the first, Deshaies stopped the Sox offense dead in its tracks. After Thomas' left center field blast, Chicago picked up only two more hits, one of them a broken bat double by Robin Ventura. Ventura's double—more luck than skill—was a blooper that barely cleared the infield.

So, Deshaies dominated the White Sox that day. Despite this domination, he lost.

The winner in this game was Sox starter Jack McDowell. He not only won 1-0, he captured his 20th win of the season in a Cy Young Award winning year. But fans at the Metrodome thought McDowell was ripe for the picking and that he would have been lucky to get past the fifth inning. The Twins teed off on McDowell. None of their hits were bleeders or bloopers or "tweeners" bouncing fifty feet in the air off the hard Metrodome AstroTurf. There were line drives everywhere, and Twins hitters looked like they knew what was coming. Any Sox fan there that day had to fear an upcoming disaster where his team would be devoured by a mud slid of runs. (It was raining rather hard outside the dome that day.)

Apparently McDowell knew what he was doing that day in Minnesota despite appearances to the contrary. The mudslide never happened. "My personality as a pitcher was that I didn't mess around," McDowell recalled to the author. "It didn't bother me that I had high ratio of hits to innings. I didn't worry about spinning a two hitter. Just keep throwing strikes and you don't get hurt." He walked only one in this game.

The game started fairly well for the Sox. Frank Thomas hit his high home run with the sound of the bat meeting the ball loudly resounding throughout the dome. The Sox had been manhandling Twins pitching and it looked like the Sox could be on their way to an easy win. As it turned out, however, nothing was easy that Sunday afternoon. Deshaies just looked sharper as the game progressed. All the Twins had to do was put a couple runs on the board, and the game was theirs.

In the second, they had men on first and second with none out. They didn't score.

In the fourth they had a man on third with one out. They didn't score.

In the sixth, they had men on first and third with none out. They didn't score.

In the seventh, they again had men on first and third with none out. They didn't score.

The seventh was truly the last stand for the Twins. David McCarty hit a double play ball. The throw to first pulled Frank Thomas off the bag; but Thomas, turning and spinning, tagged the runner out to complete the double play. He looked a like a ballet dancer. Well, sort of . . . can you imagine him pirouetting on stage in Sox pinstripes?

All tolled, the Twins had men on third with less than two outs in three innings, and all they could produce were four strikeouts and a double play. In the eighth and ninth they went three up and three down, seeming to know they had been beaten even before the last hitter struck out—McDowell's tenth strikeout. McDowell, who had looked like he was about to be knocked out of any inning, completed his own 1-0 ball game.

"Roberto Hernandez [White Sox closer in 1993] used to say," McDowell recalled, " 'Black Jack is starting today. The bullpen can take the day off.' A leader gives that type of effort. You raise the bar a little and that is what separates the great and the .500 pitcher."

McDowell was more than a .500 pitcher against Minnesota that day. It was a game that the Twins should have won and a game Jack McDowell should have lost. Yet McDowell won, demonstrating why he deserved the Cy Young Award. The Sox clinched the division a little more than a month later. It can be argued they really won it in Minneapolis the day McDowell persevered and won his 20th game.

White Sox hurler Joel Horlen talks with his wife after his no-hitter against the Detroit Tigers, September 10, 1967. Horlen had a break out year in 1967, winning 19 games while posting a 2.06 ERA. His no-hitter was not only historic, but a big win in the middle of a four team pennant race that included the White Sox, Tigers, Twins and Red Sox. Boston prevailed with only three games separating the four teams in the final standings. (Courtesy of the Gerry Bilek Photo Collection.)

One of the high points of the 1972 season, Wilbur Wood and third baseman Ed Spiezio celebrate an August 12 win over Oakland that put the White Sox in a virtual tie for first place. Wood pitched an 11-inning complete game, giving up only two hits. Spiezio hit a two-run homer in the 11th to give the Sox a 3-1 win. Spiezio was a capable replacement for the injured Bill Melton despite playing with a broken rib. Wood won his 20th game, one of four times he pulled off that feat. (Courtesy of the Gerry Bilek Photo Collection.)

Tom Seaver shows off the form that helped him win 311 games over a great career. Most of those wins came with the Mets and the Reds, but Seaver would make some history as a member of the White Sox in 1985 when he picked up win number 300. (Courtesy of the Mark Fletcher Photo Collection.)

Tom Seaver acknowledges a standing ovation from Sox fans during his first Comiskey Park appearance after notching his 300th career win. In this August 9, 1985 game, Seaver picked up his 3,500th career strikeout. (Courtesy of the Mark Fletcher Photo Collection.)

LaMarr Hoyt, the right-handed ace of the Sox staff during the early '80s, delivers from the mound. He beat the Baltimore Orioles in the '83 American League Championship Series and came oh-so-close to a perfect game in May 1984. More a pitcher than a thrower, the right-hander walked only 31 in '83. He kept hitters off balance by out-guessing them and taking what they gave him. "I would take great pleasure," Hoyt would gleefully remember, "if I had a two run lead and have a fastball hitter up there, and I know he's taking. I would throw a nice fastball straight down the middle. And he would just watch it go by. He'd be thinking, 'how did I take that pitch?'" Hoyt showed such poise during his great 1983 playoff victory, holding back Eddie Murray, Cal Ripken Jr. and the rest of the Orioles—despite having to wait out a fourth inning rain delay—for a complete game, 2-1 victory. "It was not even raining that hard," the Sox ace said, recalling how he paced the dugout. "All I did was sit back there drinking coffee and walk back and forth, just being in a little tirade myself. I just wanted to get out there and get it over with." There were no indications that the delay hurt Hoyt, tirade or not. "When I get locked in, it is hard to get locked out. I was locked in that day." (Courtesy of the Leo Bauby Photo Collection.)

34

Jack McDowell, Sox ace of the early '90s, is locked in. McDowell won the Cy Young Award in 1993 while winning 22 games. He also started the first game at New Comiskey, only to get knocked around in a 16-0 loss to Detroit. McDowell was convinced that the loss could be attributed to angering the "Gods of Old Comiskey." He and two other players burned a uniform as a sacrifice. McDowell believes the sacrifice worked. (Photo by Mark Fletcher.)

No-hit wonder, Wilson Alvarez is congratulated by catcher Ron Karkovice after throwing a no-hitter against the Baltimore Orioles on August 11, 1991. It was his first start for the Sox and only second in his major league career. Alvarez also threw a memorable complete game victory in the 1993 playoffs after the Sox had lost the first two games of the series to the Toronto Blue Jays. (Courtesy of the Gerry Bilek Photo Collection.)

THREE

Dramatic Home Runs

A walk off home run is the most emphatic play in baseball. A grand slam can change not only the outcome of the game, but also the momentum of the entire series. Baseball fans cheer for the long ball, and at Old Comiskey they would hold up bulls eyes in the bleachers to encourage their favorite South Side sluggers. From Kluszewski and Allen to Fisk and Thomas, White Sox batters have done their best since 1959 to make their fans happy, and to send them home from the ballpark with a great moment to remember, if not a souvenir.

Beating a 30-game winner
The year 1968 was a terrible.

The United States suffered through political assassinations, race riots, war, war protests, and endured a tremendous feeling of self-doubt. Most were glad when the calendar turned over to 1969. 1968 was not so hot for the White Sox, either. The team began the year with large expectations having re-acquired Luis Aparicio and also traded for two-time National League batting champion, Tommy Davis. The club had come to close to winning the pennant the previous year. It now it appeared to have enough offensive firepower to win the pennant that eluded them in another heart breaking way.

But then the season began.

The White Sox stunned and disappointed their fans with a 0-10 start. Added to the five game losing streak that ended the 1967 season, they had compiled nifty 15 game winless streak. From appearances, it looked like a World Series appearance was just a fairy tale written by a Cub fan. The only real bright spot for the Sox during the first part of the season was Pete Ward.

Ward began his White Sox career in an April 9, 1963 game against the Detroit Tigers. He came up with a key three run homer and made a good defensive play at third on a topped ball by Al Kaline to help the Sox to a 7-5 win. "It was one of the few good plays I made," Ward jokingly said about the Kaline assist and his sometime defensive lapses.

Ward was the first of three promising Sox players during an eight-year stretch to have his career hampered by an off-the-field injury. He suffered a back injury in a car accident after leaving a Black Hawks game in April 1965. His career, after starting out with two not great yet solid seasons, had taken a detour down a dark road.

After knocking out 22 and then 23 homers in his first two years, Ward only hit a combined 13 long balls during the 1965 and '66 seasons. The Sox lost an offensive threat they so desperately needed, though Ward downplays his ability as a power hitter. "I never considered myself a home run hitter," Ward told the author. "I was a line drive hitter."

That perception aside, Ward provided some clutch homers during the great pennant race of 1967. On August 16, he hit two homers and two singles in a 14-1 rout of the going-nowhere Kansas City Athletics. Two days later he came through with a two-run sixth inning round tripper off Moe Drabowksi to help beat Baltimore 3-1. On the last day of that month, Ward came through again with an eighth inning two-run shot over the bullpen in Boston to give the White Sox a 4-2 triumph over the eventual pennant winning Red Sox.

In the early stages of 1968, it looked like Ward had regained his promise of '63 and '64. After hitting two homers against Oakland on May 9, his seventh and eight of the season, Ward was actually tied for the major league lead in homers (with Roger Repoz of the Angels and the great Willie McCovey of the Giants.) Buy today's standard that doesn't appear to be much of a number. But in '68, the Year of the Pitcher, it was no small accomplishment.

However, after this power surge, Ward's power numbers dropped off. Since no one else on the Sox was hitting anything to speak of, the once perennially contending team couldn't contend for a .500 record, much less a pennant. As the season seemed to drag on, pride was all the team had left; that, and an opportunity to see if this light hitting team could derail an opposing pitcher from accomplishing an unbelievable feat.

By the time the Sox played a doubleheader against the Detroit Tigers on August 20, right-handed Tiger pitcher Denny McLain had an incredible 25-3 record. With Detroit and St. Louis not getting any serious challengers for the pennant during the last year of one-divisional play, the only suspense left was whether or not McLain would be the first pitcher in 34 years to win 30 games.

In the first game of the doubleheader, the Sox lost 7-0, managing but one hit, a fifth inning single by shortstop Ron Hansen. One would have thought that McLain had started that game, but instead it was lefty John Hiller picking up his sixth win.

Game two was unlike most White Sox games that year. They scored 10 runs, pounded out 13 hits and cruised to a 10-2 win. Sox pitcher Gary Peters, not McLain, was the star off the mound that afternoon. Peters went all the way while giving up only four hits to a team that normally provided McLain with plenty of support. McLain never got out of the sixth inning. He had some shoddy defense behind him, but he also gave up nine hits in $5^2/_3$ innings. He was chased to the showers that late summer night by a grand slam hit by Pete Ward—a 440-foot blast to the canyon known as centerfield at Tiger Stadium.

"I have no recollection of that whatsoever," Ward said in early 2004 when asked about the dramatic clout. What Ward did have was a vivid recollection of McLain picking up his 30th win on September 14 against the A's despite giving up two home runs to Reggie Jackson. "He was with us," Ward said referring to McLain's minor league days in the Sox organization. "He got me out a hell of a lot of the time. He didn't just have a fastball. He had a good curve and put it all together that year."

The homer off of McLain was one of the last Ward would ever hit for the Sox. Playing sparingly in 1969, he hit only six before he was traded to the Yankees where he finished his playing career. He led the Sox with 15 homers in 1968, not a staggering total. But his grand slam against Denny McLain was truly memorable, even if Pete Ward can't remember it.

Finally . . . 30

For Sox fans, it was a little embarrassing.

In 1970, a fan couldn't say that it had been long time since a White Sox player had hit 30 home runs in a single season. Prior to that season, *no* Sox player had hit 30 homers in a single season. The Chicago White Sox, a charter member of the American League, and a team with a history spanning seven decades, were yet to have one player break that barrier. They did have two baseball immortals—Gus Zernial and Eddie Williams—who had hit 29, but no other player who called himself a White Sox had even gotten that close. This was a dubious distinction among major league clubs.

There were several reasons for this lack of historical home run production. At the start of the century, during the "Deadball" era, nobody hit many home runs. "Home Run" Baker had a 13-year career (1908–1922) with the Philadelphia A's and the New York Yankees, picking up over 1,800 hits with a lifetime batting average of .307. But the guy who earned this powerful nickname never hit more than 12 homers in a single season and didn't even pass the 100-homer mark for his career. Hitting home runs was even frowned upon because back then the baseball world thought it took more skill to hit a single or double, to play the finesse game.

Towards the end of this era, of course, came the 1919 scandal, and the Sox were decimated talent-wise. They really didn't start winning again until the mid-1930s, and even then no one mistook them for the Bronx Bomers.

Comiskey Park was never considered a home run hitter's ballpark, either. With its expansive power alleys and over 400-foot home run barrier in center, it just didn't provide a great haven for power hitters. Sox ownership built their team around speed and pitching; the Killebrews and Aarons played for other teams.

By 1968, offensively, the team hit a real rock bottom in a league that failed to offer any significant offense. Carl Yastrzemski was the only league player who qualified for the batting title to hit .300, and he barely did that. But the Sox were truly an offensively impaired team. They hit a grand total of 71 homers, which doesn't even equal the record setting mark by Barry Bonds. In nearly 100 games, the Sox didn't hit a single homer. Fans took one good look and stayed away as the team posted the second worst record in the American League.

Meanwhile, Sox fans were looking nine miles north with envy. Banks, Williams, and Santo rocked Wrigley with power. Even though the Cubs blew a big lead in 1969, they at least entertained their fans with a team that could score runs with the long ball. The Sox hit better as a team in 1969, increasing their home run total to 112. Management had reduced the dimensions of Comiskey significantly by putting up a short fence in front of the old wall. But the dimensions, reduced from 353' to 335' down the lines, from 375' to 370' in the power alleys, and from 415' to 400' in straight away center, helped the opposition just as much as they helped the Sox. Also, any homer that fell between the new fence and old wall was a turn-off, and, in fact, an admission that the Sox couldn't hit.

Bill Melton was in his second full season in 1970. His 1969 power numbers of 23 homers and 87 RBIs were respectable. He had a break through game on June 24 of that year hitting three homers in the second game of a doubleheader against the Seattle Pilots. With Melton playing third, Sox fans hoped he would be a taller version of Ron Santo, as it was logical to hope for power from that position.

Melton struggled defensively at third in 1970 but began developing as a power hitter. The shortened dimensions helped him only a little. Most of his homers went into the upper deck or into the centerfield bullpen. He had a nice two-homer game against Boston on June 9, hitting one deep into the bullpen and another far into the lower deck, landing in one of the exit ramps. The two solo shots allowed the White Sox to win 4-2 in one of the best games they played all year.

On August 2, he hit a two-out two-run homer in the bottom of the ninth off of ex-Cub lefty Dick Ellsworth to pull out a game against the Indians. Using his upper cutting swing, Melton cleared the 400-foot marker by a good 30 or 40 feet. Historically, Sox players didn't hit with that kind of power.

Melton's development didn't draw too much attention. The Sox were horrible in 1970, and going for 30 homers was not like chasing 60. But at least he gave the few remaining diehard Sox fans something to cheer about that season.

On September 18, Melton became the third Sox player in history to hit 29 homers in a single season. It was a typical Melton blast. Picking on a high pitch from Twins reliever Ron Perranoski, Melton sent an arching drive in the second row of the left center field upper deck. He had 15 games left to hit number 30.

Again, this was not the race to 60, so the baseball world wasn't exactly holding its breath. Additionally, the Sox were so bad that many fans had already turned their attention to the Bears, a team with no quarterback and no chance to get to the NFL playoffs. The Sox played a mid-week double header against the Kansas City Royals on September 21. Kansas City was no better a draw than the Sox, and the late-season doubleheader was played during a school day.

Attendance was sparse. Only 672 fans were there, one of the smallest crowds in team history, and huge Comiskey Park offered plenty of elbowroom that sunny fall afternoon.

The old question, "If a tree falls in a forest with no one there to hear it, does it make a sound?" may be asked for that little bit of White Sox history that day. But there definitely was a sound: the sound of the ball meeting Bill Melton's bat.

Not surprisingly, the upper deck was empty. The ball hit in the middle of a vacant seat in left center and dropped back down on the field. It had taken 70 years, but a White Sox hitter finally broke the 30 home run barrier. Melton finished with 33 that year.

Melton feels that the Sox have since changed their philosophy about strictly building a team around pitching and defense. In the post-Melton years, we have seen the South Side Hit Men, and Greg Luzinksi, Harold Baines and Carlton Fisk of the Winning Ugly ball club, and Big Frank, Mags, and Carlos Lee today. Melton's single season and career Sox records have been passed time and again. But there had to be a first, and Bill Melton was the first to go where no Sox had gone before.

A Home Run Champion?

Chicago White Sox hitters and home run championships had nothing in common.

Mickey Mantle with 40, Roger Maris with 61, Harmon Killebrew with 48, 45, and 49, Tony Conigliaro with 32, Frank Robinson with 49, Killebrew and Carl Yastrzemski with 44, Frank Howard with 44, Killebrew with 49 and Howard again with 44. This is the list of home run champions in the American League from 1960 to 1970. As anyone can see, none were White Sox players. If anyone made a list going back to the beginning of baseball, none of the names would be that of a Chicago Southside ballplayer.

During the '60s, one of their biggest home run threats was pitcher Gary Peters who just didn't get enough at-bats to seriously compete for the homer run championship. (Peters hit 15 homers in his career, which isn't bad for a pitcher.) The Go-Go Sox were forever built around speed and pitching, producing some winning teams—and some real boring baseball. In 1971, that began to change.

As the season came to a close, three American Leaguers were in contention for the home run championship. With two games left on the Sox schedule, Reggie Jackson of the A's had 32 homers, Norm Cash of the Tigers also had 32, and Bill Melton of the White Sox had 30. Nothing else was at stake. The A's had already clinched their division, and the Sox were going to finish third in the West no matter what they did in their two final games against the Milwaukee Brewers.

With this scenario, Chicago manager Chuck "the glass is always half-full" Tanner inserted the slow footed, usually clean-up hitter Melton in the lead off spot. The strategy was rather simple: batting first, Melton would get more at-bats and thus more cracks at hitting home runs. And he would do only that—try to hit home runs. Many times when a hitter actually tries, it doesn't happen.

On September 29, Melton went against this trend by hitting two homers in a 2-1 win over the Brewers and rookie pitcher Jim Slaton. Both were well hit, one going into the upper deck with the other traveling well into left center. Overall, it was a great game for the Sox as Wilbur Wood picked up his 22nd win, the most wins by a Sox pitcher since Early Wynn won the same number in the pennant-winning year of 1959. However, Melton's solo blasts in the first and third innings were the real story. With these two long drives, he had assured himself of at least a tie for the championship, because Cash and Jackson finished their seasons that night without another homer.

Melton was back in the leadoff spot the next day for the season finale. The Milwaukee starter was Bill Parsons, a rookie who had a decent year for the last place Brewers. Unless the Sox did a completely inept job of hitting, the third baseman would have at least four chances to make some significant White Sox baseball history. In his first at-bat, he hit a weak looking grounder to short that would have been a great shot if he were playing miniature golf.

"Parsons shattered my bat," Melton said in describing his first attempt that day. "They [his teammates] put a towel over the bat in the dugout and gave it its last rites. I was laughing and thinking, wow, when is this going to be over? Guys were making bets. It was a lot of fun down there."

The answer came on his next at-bat. In the third inning, looking for a fastball on a 2-0 pitch, Melton got what he was looking for and ripped a drive to deep left. It as a line shot with some height to it, just missing the façade of the upper deck before landing in the lower seats. The homer was Melton's 33rd, and for the first time in team history, the Chicago White Sox had an American League Home Run Champion.

Back in the dugout, Melton thought his season was truly over. The home run title was his, the game had no further meaning, and he looked forward to getting out of the ballpark to catch a flight back to his home in California. He was somewhat shocked to find out that Manager Chuck Tanner wanted him to go back to his position at third base. He pleaded with Tanner to take him out, but Tanner wouldn't hear of it, and Melton returned to his position, though he describes his attitude as "pissing and moaning."

One out later, Tanner came on the field to take Melton out (He was replaced by fun-loving Walt "No-Neck" Williams who liked to take grounders in pre-game practices, but was no threat to the legacy of Brooks Robinson). The new American League Home Run Champion acknowledged the small, but enthusiastic crowd. He threw his hat into the stands behind the Sox third base dugout and a young, longhaired woman caught it. She jumped up and down with a real joy. It was a great moment for a player connecting with his fans at one of the true high points of his career.

Melton was grateful to Tanner, who had no intention of keeping Melton in the game beyond the first out, for sending him back out onto the field. "He [Tanner] did that as a favor to me," Melton recalled. "From what few people that were there, he wanted me to get the cheers."

Melton had achieved another White Sox first. By picking up three homers in his last six at-bats, he joined the ranks of Killebrew, Howard, Mantle, Robinson and Maris. Not bad company, indeed.

The Dramatic Bat Day Home Run, or "You're in Deep S— Now, Sparky"

Once a Dick Allen home run was seen, it was never forgotten.

There was never a real doubt about any Allen blast. The fan might be fooled briefly, but that was only by the line drive homers. Those line drives were hit so low that even the well-seasoned fan could be deceived, but that was only because one wouldn't think that a ball hit so low could travel so far. Deceived momentarily or not, utter amazement could only describe the typical reaction to a Dick Allen clout. There was something about how the ball jumped off his bat, how it soared to the deepest and farthest sections of Old Comiskey, or how his line drives ripped into the lower deck with such speed and force.

So amazed were the fans that there was a buzz throughout Comiskey every time Allen stepped up to the plate. The situation didn't have to be critical; fans simply anticipated seeing what they had seen on so few occasions from a White Sox hitter. Allen had that unique combination of hitting ability and power that made him the most feared offensive threat in the American League in 1972. That year White Sox fans latched onto Allen with more fanaticism than a rock and roll groupie.

Yet the unrealistic expectations of Allen producing every time didn't seem to faze him. His walk up to the plate was never hurried. When he didn't produce, he showed no visible signs of frustration or anger. Allen didn't throw bats or helmets, and petty arguments with umpires were beneath him. After striking out, Allen took a very casual stroll back to the dugout, bat securely tucked under his arm. He'd glance at the pitcher as if to say, "Wait till next time." Unlike the idle Cub fan threat of "Wait until Next Year," there was a next time. When the next time came, the opposition was better off ducking than trying to catch up with a drive off of Dick Allen's bat.

Allen didn't have the typical physique of a slugger. He didn't have the massive arms of a sleeveless Ted Kluszewski or the short muscular build of a Harmon Killebrew or the athletic aura of a Willie Mays. What he did have was incredibly strong wrists that moved his 40-inch, 40-ounce bat through the strike zone with great speed and power. Allen even looked impressive when striking out.

He began his career in Philadelphia in 1964 and won National League Rookie of the Year Honors when he collected 201 hits and slugged 29 homers. Known as Richie back then, Allen had what could only be described as a turbulent time in the City of Brotherly Love. Labeled as a trouble-making malcontent with no team spirit, Allen had a hate-hate relationship with Phillie fans. He began wearing a helmet even when playing the field to protect himself from feared fan projectiles and took to writing "BOO" in the infield dirt with his cleats. By the end of the 1969 season, ballplayer and fan looked forward to parting company. During one of his last games at old Connie Mack Stadium, a fan draped a huge banner over the railing of the upper deck that read, "It Won't Be Long Now, Richie!!!! (Oct. 2)"

By most reports, it appeared that Richie Allen had a newfound home in St. Louis for the 1970 season. He whacked 34 homers and knocked in 101 in the then vast Busch Stadium that was more conducive to a team with good defense, speed and pitching than a homer hitting first baseman.

But in 1971, Allen was playing for the Dodgers, now having completely moved across the country from Brooklyn to Los Angeles. St. Louis had barely waited for the 1970 season to end before sending him to Los Angeles, completing the trade on October 5. There his power numbers, 23 homers and 90 RBIs, were down but still very respectable in an era of abundant strong pitching.

Allen was still a good hitter, but Los Angeles was willing to part with him as well. The Sox traded left-handed pitcher Tommy John and unproven infielder Steve Huntz for the still controversial Allen. Sox fans were thrilled. The 1971 team had won only 79, but that was a big improvement over the awful 56-106 squad of 1970. In addition, Bill Melton had won the American League Home Run Championship, and Wilbur Wood became the first Sox pitcher to win 20 in seven seasons. It looked like the Sox could become contenders if they filled a few holes.

But Allen's joining the team was delayed. He was a no-show for spring training, as he and the White Sox still hadn't come to contract terms. Many fans feared the ugly head of Philadelphia Richie had reared up, and that all the Sox got for their trouble was the loss of a starting pitcher.

Richie Allen finally showed up as spring training ended. He signed his contract and was ready to play. The problem was that Major League Baseball wasn't ready to play. The owners and players were in the middle in one of their many labor disputes, resulting in a lockout and the season being delayed until April 15. The Sox lost a huge opening day gate and instead began their season on the road in Kansas City.

Chicago dropped the season opener 2-1, but Allen reassured fans that missing spring training did nothing to diminish his skills. He clobbered a massive homer over the left center field wall in the ninth to break a 0-0 tie. It was Chicago's first real good look at the Allen's powerful down-cutting swing.

By the time the Sox finally returned to Chicago, Allen and White Sox fans were still strangers to each other. On joining the Sox, Allen made a request to the media and the fans. He didn't want to be known as Richie as he was in Philadelphia, St. Louis and Los Angeles. He wanted to be called Dick Allen. When the media and the fans immediately agreed to this simple request, the man thought of as nothing but a troublemaker was truly flattered.

"I open the Chicago papers and there I am—Dick Allen," the slugger would tell writer Tim Whittaker. "I go to the park and everybody's calling me Dick, the ushers, the clubhouse guys, the fans. First time. First city to call me by the name my mother gave me at birth. I'd about given up. I made up my mind right then and there that Dick Allen was going to pay back Chicago for the respect they were giving me."

42

The 1972 love affair between Allen and White Sox fans was in its beginning stages. And on June 4 that relationship was cemented in a moment that only symbolized his incredible 1972 season.

June 4 was Bat Day at Old Comiskey. The Sox played a Sunday afternoon doubleheader against the New York Yankees. These Yankees were not the murderer's row of Ruth and Gehrig or of Mantle and Maris. But they were still the hated Yankees, and the Yankee name still had the power to revive memories of heartbreaking defeats and shattered World Series dreams. In fact, the previous day, New York had scored two in the ninth to tie the game and then piled on eight in the 13th to turn a hard fought game into an 18-10 rout.

Nearly 52,000 showed for that summer-like afternoon doubleheader, and the Sox responded with a 6-1 win in game one. The near capacity crowd made plenty of noise as hard throwing right-hander Tom Bradley pitched a complete game, and Bill Melton iced the win with a towering sixth inning home run deep into the lower deck, about ten feet to right of the foul pole. Dick Allen contributed to the win by stealing home in the eighth. It was one of his 19 steals that season.

But then the starting lineups were announced for game two and Dick Allen was not slotted in his usual number three spot. Not only that, Allen wasn't playing at all.

The second half of a doubleheader is not a bad time to rest a player. Allen had played in every game of the season to that point. But these were the Yankees the Sox were playing and they were doing it in front one of the largest crowds in recent team history. The 51,904 that came that day would have constituted over ten percent of the gate for the entire 1970 season. Wouldn't some Monday night have game been a better time to sit Allen down? Wouldn't Allen, choosing to rest on such a dramatic day, just fuel speculation that he was a true malcontent?

The Sox could have used Allen. Going into the ninth, Chicago trailed New York 4-2. But the Sox had two men on with one out and an extra base hit could help save the day. A homer would win it. Light hitting shortstop Rich Morales was due up, but he was called back to the bench. Popping out of the dugout was the now familiar number 15—Dick Allen—pinch-hitting.

As ever, the stadium buzzed when Allen walked up to the plate. The fans worked themselves up into their usual frenzy, but from his calm appearance this was just another at-bat for the confident Dick Allen.

Yankee manager Ralph Houk decided to bring in his ace reliever left hander Sparky Lyle. During the early and mid-'70s, the Comiskey bullpen was situated in foul territory down the outfield lines. A visiting reliever often walked past first on his way to the mound. Sox infielder Mike Andrews, who had roomed with Lyle when both played for the Red Sox, was perched on first after having just singled. Andrews felt he could get away with taunting his old friend.

"You're in deep shit now, Sparky," Andrews said referring to Lyle having to face Allen.

The first two pitches gave no indication that Sparky was indeed in deep shit. Allen took both, and worked the count to an even one-and-one. But the third Lyle offering provided for one of the most dramatic White Sox moments in the last half of the 20th century.

The line drive looked ordinary at first. It barely cleared the infield. Then it appeared to be one of those sharply hit balls to be caught by the outfielder. It continued cut through the early, heavy evening air, rising slowly but steadily. Left fielder Roy White drifted back, first to the warning track and then to the wall. His face registered half awe and half disappointment as he watched the ball tear into the waiting arms of Sox fans sitting deep in the left field seats. The Sox had beaten the once mighty Yankees 5-4.

Sox fan Mark Liptak sat in the right field stands. The ball was already in flight when he heard the crack of the bat. The sequence occurred because the speed of sound was slower. Slower yes, but very loud. Liptak said the sound resembled a "bullet shot" and he had never seen or heard a ball hit that hard.

Meanwhile, Allen, the reputed malcontent with no team loyalty, turned to his first base coach half way between first and second. He smiled widely and pumped his fist. On arriving at home plate, Allen was greeted by the entire Sox team. No longer was he Richie Allen of Philadelphia, St. Louis or Los Angeles. He was now Dick Allen of the Chicago White Sox.

According to Liptak, Sox fans didn't leave the park for another half-hour because they wanted hold onto the joy of the moment. They cheered, stamped their feet, banged on seats, not quite believing that Allen had done it again. The noise and the vibration could be heard and felt in the Sox clubhouse below the stands.

In 1972 Allen became only the fourth player to hit a home run into the center field bleachers at Old Comiskey, became only the second player in major league history to hit two inside the park homers in one game, and won the American League Most Valuable Player Award. One would like to say controversy stopped following him. He missed the last two months of the 1973 season due to injury. Some charged that the injury wasn't serious enough to sideline him, an accusation that Allen vehemently denied. He "retired" with three weeks remaining in the 1974 season, leaving Sox fans feeling deserted, and came out of this very brief retirement to return to Philadelphia of all places.

Allen left baseball for good when he walked out on the Oakland A's during the middle of the 1977 campaign. Ironically, his last game was played against the White Sox in a Sunday doubleheader on June 19. Allen and A's owner Charlie Finley had a confrontation when Allen was found showering in the middle of the second game. An angry Allen left never to return. With the two wins by Chicago that day, the Sox moved into the first place for the first time that season. White Sox fans worked themselves into the same type of excitement as they did for the 1972 Bat Day homer, and were too caught up with the South Side Hit Men to know, notice or care that their one-time idol was no longer playing Major League Baseball.

Yet in 1972, Sox player and Sox fans truly bonded in a way that hasn't been matched since. One factor contributed to this intense love affair: once a Dick Allen homer was seen, it was never forgotten.

Alone in First Place
First place.

Those two words were rarely used to describe a Chicago baseball team in the early '70s. The Cubs were at the end of their winningest stretch of baseball during the last half of the 20th century in 1972, having put together a string of six .500-plus seasons. Yet even their most loyal fans had to know that the window of opportunity had been sealed shut after the 1969 season.

From 1968 to '71, first place was not even something that was contemplated by the White Sox. After their own heartbreak of 1967, they lost the first ten games of the 1968 season, finished behind an expansion team in 1969, and had one of their worst seasons in franchise history in 1970. The South Siders rebounded somewhat in 1971, but still ended up losing more than they won. First place? You had to be kidding.

But on August 20, 1972, the Chicago White Sox actually had a chance to take over first all by themselves, depending on how they fared against the Boston Red Sox in a doubleheader. It was incredible if not unbelievable.

In game one they had Wilbur Wood on the mound. A start by Wood at Comiskey was almost an automatic win during 1972. By the beginning of the eighth, many of the over 29,000 at Comiskey Park already looked forward to the second game. It was in the bag.

The White Sox led 5-1. They got a solo home run from little shortstop Luis Alvarado, the last person fans expected to reach the seats. Granted it barely made it into the first row, with a Sox fan bear hugging the souvenir to his chest. But a home run was a home run and the scoreboard went off just the same.

Sox fans suddenly got very nervous when Boston plated three in the eighth. The usually dominating Wood got roughed up and Terry Forster relieved him. Forster did well for the most part except for wild pitching in a run. Now the laugher was no laugher as the White Sox led by a measly run.

In the Boston ninth, things worsened. Third baseman Rico Petrocelli singled in two runs with a bases load hit, and Boston led for the first time since the second inning. But it was only a one run lead, and the White Sox had a chance if Forster could get Red Sox catcher Carlton Fisk out. Fisk hit what looked like an inning ending grounder to the mighty Alvarado. The reliable shortstop should have had no problem. The earlier hero lifted his glove up too soon and the ball shot into left center field. The Red Sox had another run, and a lead that looked insurmountable. Two runs are not really insurmountable, but winning in the ninth down by two is never an easy task. And the White Sox just weren't in the practice of doing that over the past last few years.

The Sox did score with two out and had two men on in their half of the ninth. Now it was it was up to right fielder Pat Kelly to deliver a big it. Pat Kelly was a lead off man, not a RBI man; he'd get on base, steal second or third, and was there for someone else to drive him home. Kelly was a decent player in his day, but one would have liked to have someone else up in this situation. (Someone like Dick Allen.)

There was no getting around it. It was Pat Kelly or nothing. He gamely battled reliever Marty Pattin, fouling off several two-strike pitches, and then Kelly finally put the ball in play, sending a fly to center field.

It wasn't just any fly ball. It was a high and deep. Boston center fielder Tommy Harper could only watch as a spectator as the drive flew over the center field fence for a three-run homer. The White Sox, the right Sox in this case, won 9-7.

The "Sox O'Gram" on the center field scoreboard flashed the happy news. The Chicago White Sox were alone in first place in the Western Division. In August. In late August. One beer vendor was selling what he called "Pat Kelly beers." He sold quite a few.

The White Sox lost the second game of the doubleheader partly because center fielder Buddy Bradford played a single into a triple. At the end of the day they had to settle for a first place tie with Oakland. Then Oakland won the division, and the Sox wouldn't know what being in first place was really like until 11 years later.

But on August 20, 1972, none of these heart-breaking things had happened yet. Because of a dramatic home run by an unlikely hero, the White Sox were in first place. In August. In late August. For one day they made Chicago baseball history. They were in first place, really, no kidding.

Pete Ward faces off against the Washington Senators, 1968. Ward led the White Sox in home runs four times during the '60s but never truly reached his potential after an automobile accident in 1965. Notice the graceful arcing windows behind the left field seats and beauty of the trees right outside the ballpark. (Courtesy of the Gerry Bilek Photo Collection.)

Portrait of a slugger: Bill Melton follows through on swing that clinched the 1971 American League Home Run Championship on September 30. The Sox third baseman hit three homers in his last six at bats to take the title away from Norm Cash and Reggie Jackson. Melton had started and ended the 1971 season well. In an opening day doubleheader against Oakland, Melton hit a home run in each game, including a grand slam. (Courtesy of the Gerry Bilek Photo Collection.)

Bill Melton (left) is greeted by outfielder Pat Kelly after a Melton homer. (Courtesy of the Gerry Bilek Photo Collection.)

Roy Sievers was one of the veterans Bill Veeck brought onto the White Sox with dreams of another pennant. Sievers is in fine form here, belting a three-run homer against the Cleveland Indians on June 21, 1961. Sievers also clubbed a grand slam giving him seven RBIs for the night. The Sox won the game. The pennant was won by someone else. (Courtesy of the Gerry Bilek Photo Collection.)

Here is the picture perfect Dick Allen swing. His home runs were breath taking, his all around ability was something any baseball fan could appreciate, and he made 1972 a truly great White Sox season. He was a superstar that the White Sox had so desperately needed. The choice for the 1972 American League Most Valuable Player Award was an easy one. Dick Allen was only the second White Sox player to win it, the first since Nelson Fox in 1959. Fans not only came back that year, they buzzed with excitement every time Allen stepped up to the plate. Most times he didn't disappoint them. (Courtesy of the Mark Fletcher Photo Collection.)

Manager Chuck Tanner and Dick Allen talk at spring training in 1973. Tanner was called a "great handler of men" when it seemed that Dick Allen found true and long sought-after happiness with the White Sox. Others claimed the Sox manager coddled Allen. Not so, said Tanner. Tanner claimed that he didn't one set of rules for Allen and another for the other 24 players. The optimistic Sox manager said he had 25 sets of rules for 25 players. Regardless, this looks like a match made in heaven. (Courtesy of the Gerry Bilek Photo Collection.)

Pat Kelly follows through on a home run swing that won a game. Kelly knocked one over the center field fence with two outs in the ninth to pull out a victory against Boston. For a short time, before game two of that day's doubleheader was over, the White Sox had sole possession of first place. (Courtesy of the Leo Bauby Photo Collection.)

Carlton Fisk sets the record for home runs hit by a catcher. Here he is launching his 328th homer as a catcher, off Charlie Hough on August 17, 1990. His great career spanned three decades. Fisk also set the record for most games played by a catcher. He played for the White Sox from 1981 to 1993, but entered the Hall of Fame as a Red Sox. (Courtesy of the Mark Fletcher Photo Collection.)

Carlton Fisk is the greatest catcher the White Sox ever had. He is being congratulated here for setting a record for most home runs hit by catcher. He also set the record for games played at that position, and in a crazy play in 1985, tagged two runners out at the plate against the Yankees in a rather strange double play. (Courtesy of the Gerry Bilek Photo Collection.)

FOUR

Great Opening Days

Opening Day of the baseball season is always memorable. Hope springs eternal as all teams in the major leagues are—however fleetingly—tied in the standings. Season after season, Opening Day on Chicago's south side has provided its share of great moments for Sox fans, even if the ballpark was more than half empty that day and all eternal hope was to become long lost by mid-summer.

A Star is Born . . . Well Almost
1969 looked like it was going to be the Year of the Cub.

The North Side baseball team got off to a great start with a dramatic season opening win. Ernie Banks, thought to be washed up, hit two home runs, and Willie Smith won it for the Cubbies with a two-run pinch-hit homer in the eleventh. Following two moderately successful seasons in '67 and '68, the Cubs were no longer the laughing stock of Chicago and the National League. They were now contenders, and their fans had a giddiness that only Cub fans could have.

On the other side of town, the White Sox franchise was in deep trouble. 1968 ended a long string of winning seasons that had begun in 1951. Just as importantly, they had no big names, no drawing card and many aging veterans on a team that realistically was not going to contend in the first season of two-divisional play.

On April 16, 1969, that outlook changed slightly, at least in the area of having a developing player who would draw fans to the park.

The White Sox played their home opener against the newly formed Kansas City Royals that warm spring day. Carlos May, one of five young players who had been inserted into an overhauled lineup after the disaster of 1968, led off and played left field. The brother of power-hitting Lee May of the Cincinnati Reds, Carlos was not a known commodity to Sox fans at the start of 1969 season. He had been up briefly in late '68 but had only 67 official at-bats, hitting much like the rest of the Sox lineup—weakly.

Yet from the very start, May began to show Sox fans that he was a different type of hitter. Chicago began their season on the West Coast. May hit two solo homers (almost an unheard of event from Sox players during the late '60s) in a 3-0 win over Oakland. The left fielder also drove in the third run with a single. A few days later he picked up a double off of knuckleballer Hoyt Wilhelm in an eighth inning rally to help defeat the Angels.

The Sox recognized that they weren't going to win or draw fans without more hitting, and so the team made two significant changes to Comiskey Park in 1969. Astroturf was installed in the infield to help ground balls skip into the outfield for base hits. Secondly, a short, padded cyclone fence was erected in front of the old brick wall to shorten the home run dimensions. As it turned out, May didn't need any help from pulled in fences during the home opener.

Placed in the leadoff spot, he began the Sox home season with an opposite field homer to left. The drive sailed deep into the seats almost straight down the left field line, just a few feet to the right of what would have been the 353 mark.

In the fifth, May homered into the center field bullpen for two more runs. It is hard to say if it would have cleared the old 415 mark, but, regardless, it was a 400 foot-plus shot helping the Sox to a 5-2 victory. The season wasn't even two weeks old, and May had already pulled off two two-homer games. Could the Sox honestly have a guy who could hit? From the way the ball jumped off of Carlos May's bat, it appeared that they did.

As the season progressed the stocky and muscular May demonstrated that his opening day heroics were no fluke. On June 3, he hit a grand slam off of Boston left-handed reliever Sparky Lyle to help the Sox win a nationally televised night game 6-4 at Fenway. By the All-Star break, May had 17 homers and 57 RBIs. In 1967 and '68, Pete Ward led the Sox in those departments by amassing 18 homers and 62 RBIs and 15 homers and 50 RBIs, respectively, for those entire seasons.

May was the only Sox representative on the American League All-Star Team, drawing the attention of Washington Senator manager Ted Williams. "He's a real slasher—a real ripper like Stan Musial was," Williams said. "He'll be a big star in this league before he is through."

Yes, he looked like the real thing. But a few weeks after the All-Star game, May had an accident cleaning out a mortar while serving in the Army reserves. He lost half of his thumb and was done for the 1969 season. Worse yet, it was feared that May would never play again.

May rebounded with a .285 mark in 1970; hit an inside-the-park grand slam against the Angels in September, 1971; had a career high average of .308 in 1972; and led the Sox with 20 homers and 96 RBIs in 1973. However, he had to drastically change his batting style because of the loss of half of his thumb. Carlos May never truly realized the full potential and promise of the talented, raw rookie who had hit two homers on opening day at Old Comiskey in April 1969.

Still, his comeback was more than inspiring, and there was yet another great moment for Carlos May on Opening Day at Comiskey in 1970. Although the Sox drew only a little over 11,000 for their first home game, the fans were an enthusiastic bunch. When May took his first step into the batter's box since his injury, the crowd gave him a standing ovation. So moved by this show of affection, May had to step out of the box to compose himself.

Opening Day Excitement
The Sox were in a funk.

After three straight miserable seasons, very few Sox fans had high hopes for their team's 1971 prospects. Yes, the young team had talent in spots, but as their recent record indicated, it was only in spots. Besides, after losing 106 games in 1970, one would figure the team had to improve somewhat. No team could be that bad two seasons in a row, could they?

Chicago was also in a sports funk. Any time a Chicago team got close to winning something big, it usually found some way to fail. Many worried that the city franchises had a serious case of "chokeitis," ready to let their fans down just as it would appear true success was there for the taking. The Cubs and their fans still felt the effects of 1969. The Bears, given a chance to go the playoffs in 1968, lost the last game of year to the despised Packers by one point. The Monsters of the Midway then managed but one win in 1969. The Bulls actually were a very good team, but they couldn't get to the NBA Finals, and wouldn't until fairly deep into the Jordan era. The Black Hawks were ending their glorious time as a NHL power, and lost the 1971 Stanley Cup by making two very human mistakes in the last two games against Montreal. The 1963 Bears NFL championship was starting to look lonely and isolated amidst all the losing.

Why invest any emotion in the White Sox, a team that still seemed to be on the decline, even after losing 106 games? Fans didn't come by these hardened feelings overnight. Since the five game losing streak that ended 1967, the Sox were barely competitive.

A few weeks before the 1970 season ended, owner John Allyn changed the face of his front office and field management team. Gone were Manager Don Gutteridge and General Manager

Ed Short. Chuck Tanner was named manager and Roland Hemond took over the GM duties. The changes were necessary if not overdue.

Roland Hemond wasted little time making significant changes of his own. Between October 1970 and Opening Day 1971, Hemond traded Gail Hopkins, John Matias Ken Berry, Sid O'Brien, Jose Ortiz, Luis Aparicio, Barry Moore, Jerry Janeski, Tommy McCraw, Duane Josephson and Danny Murphy. In return the Sox acquired Pat Kelly, Don O'Reilly, Mike Andrews, Luis Alvarado, Jay Johnstone, Tom Egan, Tom Bradley, Dave Lemonds, Pat Jacquez, Bill Robinson, Rick Reichardt, Vicente Romo, Tony Muser, and Ed Stroud. Although many of these names were not known by the casual baseball fan, many were long time Sox players whose leaving signified a real change for the club. Also, many of the new Sox additions made at least short-term impacts that led to a more competitive team.

Still, after three straight seasons of lousy baseball, the 1971 White Sox had far to go before convincing a skeptical fan base that the team was at least entertaining, and worth the price of admission. Spending another year at the bottom of the standings would not win over a championship-starved following. The White Sox took some steps to regain credibility and win back some fans for the home opener.

There was a power shift in American League West in 1971. Minnesota had won the first two division titles fairly easily after being one of the top American League teams during the '60s. However, the Twins were aging as all teams eventually do, and a younger team was ready to step up as a division and World Series contender. Winning 89 the year before, and sporting the likes of Reggie Jackson, Sal Bando, Jim "Catfish" Hunter, Rollie Fingers and Joe Rudi, the Oakland A's were considered the new real power of the West. Oakland was where the Sox started their season.

A's owner Charlie Finley liked to look for new ways to spice up baseball. Colorful uniforms and teams helped; a pinch running specialist and orange baseballs didn't. In 1971, Finley came up with another unique idea, and on the surface, it was an interesting one. He had his A's open their season with something that had not been tried before, an opening day doubleheader. The White Sox were the guinea pigs in this experiment.

Also, it appeared that the Sox would be the perfect lab experiment. Not only were they miserable in 1970, their doubleheader record that year was atrocious. It was a perfect scenario for the A's to get a great start to their division title run.

In game one, it appeared the plan was working beautifully for Oakland as the A's jumped out to a 4-0 lead. But a two-run homer by Bill Melton started the Sox comeback. Down 5-4 in the top of the seventh, pinch hitter Rich McKinney singled in the tying run with two outs. The ball skipped past center fielder Rick Monday and the far from fleet-footed Ed Herrmann scored from first with what proved to be the go ahead run. The Sox won 6-5.

Carlos May did what only a Chicago baseball player could do when he homered in game two only to be called out on the play. May, high fiving a teammate, didn't look down and missed home plate. (Still hard to do.) Oakland noticed and tagged May, and the home run became a triple and an out.

The May miscue didn't matter. Melton hit a grand slam, and the newly acquired Jay Johnstone and Mike Andrews also homered. Game two wasn't even close as the Sox coasted behind the complete game pitching of Bart Johnson to a 12-4 win. The 23,823 A's fans in attendance probably went home thinking they could do without Charlie Finley and his bright ideas.

As for the Sox fans, few expected their heroes to come home from a triumphant West Coast trip, even a two-game trip. Sox management hoped their Opening Day crowd would hit the 25,000 mark, about 5,000 less than their last three home openers combined.

April 9, 1971, was a cool, overcast day. Their opponent was the defending division champion Twins. From early indications, it looked like Comiskey would have a decent but not overwhelming crowd. But the park kept swelling with people and suddenly it was hard to spot an empty seat. The Sox, unprepared for the crowd that totaled 44,250, ran out of concessions by the fourth inning.

55

By the time the White Sox came up in the bottom of the first, the crowd was buzzing with an excitement that hadn't been experienced in years. With two outs, Mike Andrews ripped a double down the left field line. Melton followed with another line shot only to have it speared by third baseman Harmon Killebrew.

Sox fans got their first look at starting pitcher Tom Bradley that day. Bradley came to Chicago in the deal with the Angels that also netted Jay Johnstone. A month shy of his 24th birthday, the large glasses wearing Bradley looked more like a geeky professor than overpowering major league pitcher. Looks can be and were deceiving, as the young right-hander was truly overpowering that afternoon. Bradley struck out future Hall of Famer Killebrew twice that day—once on blistering fastball that Killebrew attacked with a vicious cut only to walk back to the dugout with bat in hand. Killebrew had come in the game with 488 career homers at a time when hitting 500 homers meant something.

It was all so different than the previous season. In 1970, if the starting pitcher got by the first inning without giving up a run, it was considered as a true accomplishment. And 44,250 fans? It had reached the point that a lengthy home stand was needed to equal that amount.

Going into the bottom of the ninth, the game was tied at 2. The Sox had a man on third with one out, and the packed stadium worked itself up again. "Bee Bee" Richard stepped up to the plate with a chance to make a great impression on Sox fans. Shortstop Richard, another new arrival, was supposed be brimming with talent and potential as a lead off hitter and base stealer. But he had gotten off to a bad start by getting picked off first in the first. He didn't fare much better in the ninth inning when he took a called third strike in a clutch situation.

Now it would take more than a fly ball to bring in the winning run. Rich McKinney came in to pinch hit. McKinney looked like a hitter. Though he hit just .168 in 119 at-bats for the Sox in 1970, McKinney had a beautiful swing and imposing batting stance. He held the bat down at the bottom and the thick end seemed to stick way up in the air. In this pinch-hitting role, McKinney didn't just look like a hitter.

It is hard to describe how hard the ball was whacked. The best thing to say is it got to left field in a flash, hitting the ground with such force that it got to outfielder Caesar Tovar as if it was bounding off cement. The big time single gave the Sox a 3-2 victory and a 3-0 start to the 1971 season.

The level of noise at Comiskey was more than deafening; it was exhilarating. Intense emotion like this at the south side ballpark was truly hard to recall. From 1968 to 70, the Sox stunk. They contended until the end in 1967, yet their 2-1 and 1-0 wins just weren't overly exciting. In the early part of the '60s the Yankees extinguished any potential excitement with late inning rallies and Sox disappointments. But for one day, April 9, 1971, hope truly sprung eternal. Several hundred fans ran on the field, and the Sox could only stand by watching as happy people slid into bases and ran themselves silly. Under the stands, people didn't want to leave. They laughed and screamed and bonded with each other. The Sox were only 3-0, but now there was hope; hope where so many other Sox teams had failed; hope where all other recent Chicago teams had failed. For one day, all the problems the Sox had faced and not overcome since the late 1967 collapse were forgotten. They looked like a real team. They looked like contenders.

Alas, Chicago was not a real contender. The White Sox lost their next seven and never were a real threat in the Western Division. They beat Oakland to start the season, but it was the A's who took the crown as expected. The title was the first of five straight for the west coast team.

The White Sox finished $22^{1}/_{2}$ games behind the A's and four games under .500. One million, at the least, was the attendance goal for major league teams that year. The Sox drew fewer than 840,000. However, they did win 23 more than the previous season—no small feat. (Chuck Tanner tried to say they actually won more. It must have been a new math.) Though their attendance figure looks less than impressive, even by 1971 standards, the team increased their gate by almost 340,000 over the previous year. 1971 was an important year in keeping the team afloat.

Then there was the opening day. April 9, 1971, ranks near the top in the last 45 years as one of the best days the franchise experienced. No division title was clinched that day, and no one did anything truly historical. Yet, it was an important day because it was step one in getting fans interested in the team once more. For one day there was hope again, a real hope of a storied franchise that finally seemed to have a future after three straight years of taking numerous steps backwards.

Saving the Sox

The year 1976 doesn't go down as a great season.

The Sox finished in last place, and if they didn't give up during the last month of the season, it looked like they did, making a valiant effort to lose 100 games. (They fell three short.) No Sox player threatened to win the home run or batting championship, and no one on the pitching staff was mistaken for a Cy Young Award candidate. Any chance the team had for a respectable year vanished when Wilbur Wood's knee was shattered by a line drive off the bat of Ron LeFlore on May 9. Wood was done for the season, and really done for his career.

Yet there was something special about Opening Day at Comiskey in 1976. After the 1975 season, it looked like the Sox would leave Chicago. For years, there had been rumors of the Sox moving, but in late 1975 it appeared that a Sox move to Seattle was more than a rumor. Owner John Allyn didn't have any money (not that he ever did in relative terms) and attendance had fallen under 800,000. No local buyer was interested in a losing club with an outdated stadium. Roland Hemond had described the situation in 1970 as "just plain bad" with the team having little talent, little money and no farm system. He felt that the situation in 1975 was just as bad.

Bill Veeck headed up a group to buy the team. At first, the American League owners wouldn't approve the sale, saying the one-time Sox owner didn't have the finances to buy and operate a major league franchise. Finally on December 10, 1975, Veeck submitted a new financial package, and he was back in baseball.

Bill Veeck was the one responsible for the vines and still hand-operated scoreboard at Wrigley Field. He put names on the backs of uniforms, and introduced the exploding scoreboard. He was a promotional wizard, packing in crowds in Cleveland during the late '40s, and at this writing, the last Chicago baseball owner to take a team to the World Series.

But to others he was the one who cheapened baseball by having a midget pinch-hit, ruined the Sox in the early '60s by trading young talent for a bunch of players on the downside of their careers, and shouldn't have taken too much credit for the 1959 World Series. While he answered his own phone and portrayed himself as a fan-friendly owner, Veeck was derided by critics as a con man that smiled as he separated people from their money through goof ball promotions and sub-par baseball teams.

One thing was not debatable on April 9, 1976: The White Sox were still in Chicago. They could have been somewhere else, and the 40,318 who showed that day knew it. About an hour before game time, Bill Veeck walked through the lower stands on the third base side. Fans left their seats to greet him, shaking his hand and patting him on the back. Hardly anyone watching couldn't be moved.

In 1976 our country celebrated its bicentennial year. Suffering from traumas of Vietnam and Watergate, Americans wanted to regain their confidence. Veeck got into the spirit of things when he hobbled onto the field with his wooden peg leg as part of a fife and drum corp in pre-game ceremonies. He was the only owner who could have pulled a trick like that.

Almost everything in the game went perfect. Wilbur Wood looked he did in 1971, pitching a complete game shutout. New Sox first baseman Jim Spencer hit a two run homer to right in the fifth inning. The scoreboard celebration was a dud when the fireworks didn't shoot off. In a way it was almost fitting that the scoreboard failed. (In that year the scoreboard was again true entertainment. Because of money constraints, John Allyn had cut back on scoreboard home run celebrations turning the once crowd pleasing entertainment into a real dud.)

The year 1976 was all down hill from there. After a somewhat decent start, the club slid downward until it reached last and stayed there. Some of the players didn't even pretend to care, and part of the Chicago media described Manager Paul Richards as a lonely man stuck in a job that no longer suited him. Still, the opening day brought some hope that had been missing from the franchise since the rebuilding of the late '60s and early '70s had failed to deliver a championship. Just maybe Veeck could turn the team around, and just maybe the White Sox would stay in Chicago for a long time.

Another New Era

At least the uniforms were cool, sort of.

To be a Sox fan during the last part of the '70s was not a real fun experience. Unable to keep the South Side Hit Men intact, Bill Veeck tried the desperate and economic way to field a baseball team. The result was three straight losing seasons where Disco Demolition proved to be the strongest memory and a dubious legacy.

The White Sox had a recurring problem during the late '70s, and that was the absence of everyday impact players. There just weren't any big names on the club, providing very little reason for any sane fan to want to come out to the park. Chet Lemon was a good and developing player, but he alone was not a real drawing card.

When his group bought the White Sox from Bill Veeck in January 1981, Jerry Reinsdorf spoke of building a strong team by developing a solid farm system. Not necessarily a bad philosophy, but it was not what many Sox fans wanted to hear at that moment. They listened to the lack of money argument for almost an entire decade, and they wanted to hear someone to say that money would be spent immediately to improve the team. Youth movements weren't high on their list.

In February 1981, Carlton Fisk became a free agent when the Red Sox did not postdate a contract to the catcher on time. Whether the error was intentional or a real piece of incompetence, Fisk now had the freedom to sign with another club. Fisk was a prototype catcher that had been a part of Red Sox nation since his first appearance in late 1969 though his first real full season was in 1972 when he won American League Rookie of the Year Honors. His biggest moment came when he homered to force a seventh game with the Cincinnati Reds in the 1975 World Series. Few fans will forget his coaxing a high drive off the foul pole in the 12th inning of what many consider one of most exciting games in World Series history. He was just the type of player the Sox needed to establish credibility with a fan base that had tired of a no-name, losing team. He signed with his new Sox, the White Sox, on March 18, 1981.

Ironically, his first game as a member of the Chicago American League team was against his old team, Boston, at Fenway Park on April 10, 1981.

The White Sox trailed 2-0 after Dennis Eckersley had pitched seven strong innings. Outfielders Bobby Molinaro and Ron LeFlore were on base with one out in the eighth. Bob Stanley was on the mound, having come in to relieve Eckersley. Swinging at the first pitch, Fisk launched a high drive over the Green Monster to give the White Sox a 3-2 lead. They would win 5-3.

The game had played out like a fairy tale. "You always fantasize that the game may turn out the way it did, but you never think it is going to," Fisk said. What he didn't know was the happy endings weren't quite over.

In the White Sox home opener, Fisk hit a fourth inning grand slam off of Brewers starting pitcher Pete Vuckovich to cap a six-run inning and lead Chicago to a 9-3 win. Not disappointed were the 51,560 fans that showed for the game, the biggest crowd since the home opener in 1978. Of course, that year the fans still were on a high from the South Side Hit Men.

In the space of four days and two games Fisk already demonstrated that the White Sox made the right decision in aggressively going after a free agent rather hoping fans would have patience for another rebuilding effort. Fisk would remain a catching constant on the team for 12 more years even though several attempts were made to move him out. He is a Sox legend in two towns.

Astroturf is being installed in the infield for Opening Day, 1969. Like the pulled-in outfield fences, the Astroturf was meant to help the Sox offense. There was no real indication that it ever did. (Courtesy of the Leo Bauby Photo Collection.)

The White Sox hoped that shorter dimensions would help their weak-hitting team get more home runs. Walt Williams makes a nice running catch of a fly ball off the bat of Yankee Roy White. Nothing looked dumber than the little league looking fence in front of the old brick wall. It didn't help much, either. (Courtesy of the Mark Fletcher Photo Collection.)

Here is a side of the fence erected in front of the old wall. (Courtesy of the Leo Bauby Photo Collection.)

Carlos May, after coming back from his military injury, receives a standing ovation from the Opening Day crowd in 1970. The left fielder was overwhelmed by the well wishes from the fans. He had a nice comeback season that year with a .285 average, though his home run total dropped. Injury, or no injury, he could still put a charge into the ball. (Courtesy of the Mark Fletcher Photo Collection.)

Carlos May makes contact on the road. One interesting note about Carlos is that he may have been the only major leaguer to wear his birth date on his jersey—May 17. (Courtesy of the Mark Fletcher Photo Collection.)

Tom Bradley faces Reggie Jackson in 1971 or '72. Bradley struck out over 200 hitters in each of his seasons with the Sox. He also put on a stellar performance in the 1971 home opener though he didn't get the win. (Courtesy of the Leo Bauby Photo Collection.)

Stu Holcomb beams as he stands between the new Sox brain trust, Roland Hemond (left) and Chuck Tanner. The two helped lead the resurgence of the team in 1971. (Courtesy of the Leo Bauby Photo Collection.)

Rich McKinney takes batting practice in spring training. Pinch-hitting in the bottom of the ninth in the Sox home opener in 1971, McKinney showed how that practice made perfect. (Courtesy of the Leo Bauby Photo Collection.)

John Allyn passes the keys to new owner Bill Veeck, December 1975. (Courtesy of the Leo Bauby Photo Collection.)

Bill Veeck is seen with His Honor on Opening Day 1976. Richard J. Daley was often called the number one Sox fan in the city. He would never attend another Sox opener. He died on December 22, 1976. (Courtesy of the Leo Bauby Photo Collection.)

Wilbur Wood shows off his form on Opening Day 1976. Looking like his old self, he shut out the Angels 4-0 in a game that signified new hope for Sox fans. (Courtesy of the Leo Bauby Photo Collection.)

It was a publicity stunt that only Bill Veeck could have pulled off. Taking part of the opening day activities, Veeck (far right) showed his Bicentennial spirit by taking the field as a part of the fife and drum corp. Imagine any current Chicago sports owner trying to do something like that today. (Courtesy of the Leo Bauby Photo Collection.)

The torch is passed once more. This time Bill Veeck is handing the team over to Jerry Reinsdorf. (Courtesy of the Leo Bauby Photo Collection.)

Carlton Fisk during Opening Day introductions, 1981. It was his first appearance at Old Comiskey Park, and he celebrated it in a grand way. (Courtesy of the Leo Bauby Photo Collection.)

Carlton Fisk follows through on grand slam home run on Opening Day, 1981. (Courtesy of the Leo Bauby Photo Collection.)

FIVE

If You Have a Sense of Humor

It's no surprise that this chapter has the most entries. Sometimes, you've just got to laugh. Unfortunately, Chicago White Sox fans know this all too well.

Play It Again, Sam

Ninety-eight wins were just not enough.

During the first half of the 1960s, the White Sox had an old and recurring problem: The New York Yankees. The Yankees were not a problem in every way. Their lineup of superstars was a great draw at Old Comiskey. Trouble was that the Yankees usually beat the Sox in those encounters, like they did in a doubleheader on August 18, 1963. In front of 44,659, they swept the Sox 8-2 and 8-4. Game set and match went to New York as the Yankees went to their fourth consecutive World Series. At the end of the season the second place White Sox were not that close, finishing eight games back, despite winning 94.

In 1964, it looked like things might be different. When the Yankees visited Comiskey for a four game series starting on August 17, only three and half games separated the Sox, New York and the Baltimore Orioles. The Yankees were actually the third place team in this race. At that point, the Bronx Bombers didn't appear invincible. Perhaps their string of championships would end, and even if the Sox didn't win the prize, it would be great if somebody else won it for a refreshing change.

Unbelievably, the Sox swept the Yankees, 2-1, 4-3, 4-2, and 5-0. New York was still in third, now $4^1/2$ games behind the first place White Sox. Chicago had a record of 75-47, a mark any team would kill for in the later stages of August. Beating the World Champions four straight was also an accomplishment, especially for a Chicago White Sox team that always seemed to be looking up.

"I've been in baseball 40 years and no series has given me more satisfaction than the one we've just taken from the Yankees," Manager Al Lopez said of the last games that the Sox played New York that year. "This was such a big series for us that my thoughts of a pennant are high now . . . I'm glad we have the Yankees out of the way. When you are ahead of them in the race you can say that."

Then a funny thing happened, and as usual, the joke was on the White Sox.

After the Yankees suffered this rare humiliation at the hands of the Sox, they boarded their team bus happy to leave Chicago behind. Fill-in infielder/outfielder Phil Linz sat in the back and decided to give the team a concert with harmonica. The baseball player/musician treated his teammates and coaches to his rendition of "Mary Had A Little Lamb."

Manager Yogi Berra, never accused of being cultured, told Linz to knock it off with the entertainment. Not hearing his skipper, Linz asked Mickey Mantle what Berra had said. Mantle replied that Yogi wanted him to play louder. Not one to defy authority, Linz did just that. He was lucky that Berra, already in a bad mood because of an almost history-making whooping by the Sox, didn't kill him with his bare hands, though the Yankee skipper made some not so subtle threats. (Subtlety was not one of Berra's better none traits.)

One would think that the Yankees might finally crumble under the weight of their recent loses, third place standing and this rather unfortunate misunderstanding. They didn't. Linz's unintended defiance had fired up the Yankee manager, who in turn fired up his team to finish up the season on a roll. They won 30 out of their last 43 and took the pennant—for the fifth consecutive time.

Can Sox fans say their team blew it Chicago baseball style? Not really. Chicago finished the year with 98 wins, including their last nine in a row. The Sox were not eliminated until the second to the last day of the season. They finished one game behind New York with the second best record in Major League Baseball. In the wild card days of the 21st century, the Sox would have been a shoe-in for the playoffs. In one divisional play of 1964, they got nothing but the sickening feeling of losing to the Yankees yet again after it appeared that they had finally won. Their only consolation was watching New York lose to St. Louis in the World Series in seven games.

And just who was this Phil Linz guy? He was called super-sub because he could fill in at many positions. His lifetime stats were not so super. He hit a total of 11 homers in seven seasons and had a career batting average of .235. The normally offensively impaired Sox had a lot of guys who could hit better than him. Yet he beat them and he beat them in a way that could have not been anticipated or imagined.

"Mary Had a Little Lamb." Couldn't this guy have done anything better than that? Too bad that "Stairway to Heaven" was still a decade away.

Humiliating Someone Else Besides Yourself
Maybe they should have played in Triple-A.

When you are a very bad baseball team, there are only a few ways you can win. One, you can play out of character and beat the opposition with a well-executed effort. Two, you can figure out what teams are worse than you, schedule as many games with them as possible and beat them. Three, catch a team on a bad day, beat them, and claim it was a well-executed effort.

In 1970, they Sox couldn't execute, so the first option had its severe limits. The second option was also not possible since the White Sox were the worst team in the league in 1970, maybe the worst in baseball. Also a team has to accept the schedule the league gives them. You can't schedule 50 games with Milwaukee just because it might make life easier. Finally, there was option three: Catch another team on a bad day and bask in their ineptitude. The White Sox did exactly that on May 31, 1970.

Nothing went right for Boston that day at Fenway Park. The Red Sox used six pitchers and gave up 22 runs on 24 hits. Carl Yastrzemski, the future Hall of Fame left fielder, dropped a fly ball with the bases loaded and two out in the first, letting three runs score. They lost rather easily despite picking up 13 runs and 16 hits themselves.

The White Sox scored six in the first, one in the third, three in the fourth, one in the fifth, seven in the sixth and four in the eighth. Luis Aparicio, Walt Williams, Bill Melton and Duane Josephson combined for a total of 16 hits, with Aparicio and Williams picking up five each. It was a moral victory for Boston when an inning went by and the White Sox didn't score.

Yet the Sox couldn't avoid some embarrassment. Although Jerry Janeski looked like a promising right-hander, that day the young pitcher couldn't pitch the required five innings for a starter to pick up the win despite being given a 10-2 lead. In fact, Boston narrowed the gap to 11-7 before the Sox broke things open with their seven run sixth.

Floyd Weaver earned the win for the Sox. Weaver looked just as bad as everyone else, giving up six runs and nine hits in five innings pitched. He also threw two wild pitches. It would be one of four career wins for Weaver in a career that spanned four seasons with four different teams, and 85 lifetime appearances.

The total runs scored in the game was the second highest in major league history. Only one pitcher, Ken Brett, who would later pitch for the White Sox, got into the game without giving up a run. Brett faced a total of two batters. For the White Sox it was their third win in their last 15 tries. In the next game, they went right back to losing.

But apparently they liked Boston because they again beat the Red Sox 13-5 on August 19. Again playing at Boston, Chicago scored 11 in the last inning to completely turn the game around, ending a six game losing streak. Too bad they couldn't play Boston more often in 1970; they might have avoided losing 100 games. Then again, even with these two wins, the White Sox were 4-8 against Boston that season.

There's Nothing Like a Split
"I detest doubleheaders."

This quote is attributed to the plain speaking White Sox manager Eddie Stanky in 1967. The Sox had traveled to Kansas City to play the Athletics just before the A's moved to Oakland. In the last stages of a pennant race, the Sox hoped they could crush the then lowly A's and position themselves for a great finish at home in a three game series against the not too mighty Washington Senators. Chicago had a brief stay in Kansas City for a two game set. Rain postponed the first game, forcing the Sox to play a twin bill. Stanky rightly feared this scenario since beating a major league team twice on the same day is always hard. To make matters worse, it was the Sox who got swept on a day known to their fans as "Black Wednesday." Their pennant dreams vanished and at this writing are still nothing but dreams.

In 1970, the White Sox didn't resemble any kind of pennant contender. They began the season badly losing their opening game 12-0 at a cold Comiskey Park. The game wasn't as close as the score might indicate.

As in Kansas City, things only worsened. The team showed it could hit some, but it also showed it had no starting pitching, no relief pitching, and a defense that was sometimes outright embarrassing. Bill Melton lost concentration getting under a foul pop up and let it hit him in the face. Center fielder Buddy Bradford made a long run for a fly only to let it go off his glove and over the center field fence for a three-run homer. Bradford added about ten feet to that drive. Other memories, many too painful to recall, are simply suppressed.

In 1970, the Sox didn't just lose single games; they lost doubleheaders. They lost them to contending teams and second year expansion teams. They lost in close games, and they were annihilated in others. They lost in a regulation nine innings and in extra innings. They lost in warm and cold, darkness and light. They lost when Don Mincher of the A's deposited a home run on right center field roof at Comiskey. They lost when Kansas City pitcher Jim Rooker picked up 5 RBIs to help the Royals complete a doubleheader sweep. They just lost, lost, lost, lost, lost, lost and lost.

Count the number of times the word lost is written in the previous sentence. The number is seven, which are how many consecutive doubleheaders the Sox lost. That clump of 14 losses made things a little difficult to contend for a division title, not that the team had any delusions. One of the marketing slogans for the team in 1970 was "Angry Young Men." They had to be angry after losing doubleheader after doubleheader. Or, as Bill Melton would put it years later in referring to the mounting losses and small home crowds, "It's hard getting humiliated before 5,000 people."

On May 17, the Sox and Royals played a Sunday doubleheader that finished off a four game set. A crowd of over 18,000 showed, a good number for a team accustomed to crowds not breaking five figures. The Sox actually had been playing better, having won four in a row and were now within two games of .500. Team owner John Allyn was elated as he saw a rare decent crowd make its way into the old stadium. "I hope we can give them a good show," Allyn said. "If we play well, we'll draw, I'm certain of that."

The results in game one and two? As you probably already guessed, they lost and lost. Most fans didn't come back in 1970. Many of the ones who did were on medication.

On June 28, the Sox played the Twins in another dreaded doubleheader, losing game one 9-1. They also lost 9-1 the previous day. There was no reason to believe they wouldn't lose again 9-1. After all, this was a doubleheader, and the Sox were already on a roll. Then a miracle happened: They won. Not the pennant, of course, just one game of a doubleheader. They tried to lose, they really did. The once proud pitching staff gave up 10 more runs, running the three game total to Minnesota to 28. But the 1970 team had occasional eruptions of power, and this power helped them not lose their eighth straight doubleheader.

In the sixth inning, the great Jim Kaat was on the mound for the Twins. The left-handed Kaat would win 283 lifetime games. On his way to this considerable achievement, Kaat struck out Carlos May and picked up the 1,500th strikeout of his great career.

Bill Melton was the next hitter and the Sox third baseman worked the count to 3 and 0. Manager Don Gutteridge gave his clean up hitter the green light to swing; probably figuring he had nothing to lose. The Sox were already 0-15 in doubleheader play. Melton hit a drive toward the left field upper deck. Camera work was not what it is today, and the WFLD camera could not keep track of the very high fly. The TV screen showed fans in the upper deck pointing up, but there was no sight of the home run. Melton claims the drive lodged itself in the gutter of the stadium roof.

Along with Melton's prodigious blast, the Sox hit three other homers. One was clubbed by Danny Murphy, a relief pitcher. Murphy had been part of the trade that sent the legendary Nelson Fox to the still new Houston Colt .45s in late 1963 and actually broke into baseball as a Cub outfielder during the early '60s. Still knowing how to handle a bat, the left handed Murphy hit a rope of a liner into the second row seats, almost skimming against the foul pole as it cleared the old brick wall.

Murphy was an unlikely hero that day. He finished that season with a 5.67 ERA and never pitched for the Sox again. But that day he put in four strong innings, allowing only three hits and one run. His home run, his first since 1961, was also very much needed. The Sox eked out the victory 11-10.

"We won't lose another doubleheader all season," Don Gutteridge happily predicted. Well, he was a little wrong about that. The Sox lost their next doubleheader against Milwaukee and the next one after that to Kansas City. All in all they would lose 12 doubleheaders in 1970, and ended up a not too hot 11-31 in twinbill play.

On June 28, 1970, however, it was time to celebrate. Happy that they didn't have to cope with the embarrassment and disappointment of yet another double loss, the Sox set off the fireworks on their scoreboard after the game. Most teams like to truly celebrate by saying, "We're Number One." On that Sunday evening, the White Sox could say with a huge relief, "We didn't lose two today." Even better yet, they didn't take the advice of Ernie "let's play three" Banks up on the North Side.

Harry Caray and the Fish Net Home Run
They don't make 'em like this anymore.

Harry Caray has for so long been associated with the Cubs it almost forgotten that he worked for two of the Cubs' archrivals. For 25 years Caray was the voice of St. Louis Cardinals. He then worked in radio and TV for the Chicago White Sox from 1971 to 1981. The seventh inning stretch sing along began with the Sox, not the Cubs; the Cubs took a fun moment and turned it into a chance for some media hound celebrity to humiliate him or herself.

By 1971 the Chicago White Sox needed something to revive their drab broadcasting team. Bob Elson was a great one at one time, but time had passed him by. His totally laid back style wasn't in vogue anymore, so he was let go after the 1970 season. To make matters worse for the Sox, no major radio outlet wanted to carry their games. Harry Caray was reduced to working on two low wattage suburban stations.

There was no bigger antipathy to Elson than Caray. Anything but laid back, there was nothing quiet about Caray. He wore loud clothing and pounded Budweisers or Falstaffs during broadcasts. More importantly, he loudly sounded like a frustrated fan, especially when a power hitter failed to deliver in the clutch. "Popped it up," the exasperated Caray would say, "that wouldn't be a home run in a phone booth."

The hard drinking Caray easily overshadowed the easy going TV play-by-play man Jack Drees and an ever-changing list of Drees' sidekicks in the Sox broadcast booth from 1968 to '72. Not shy about criticizing the team, Caray did a good job of promoting himself as a fan-friendly announcer. Tough-to-please Sox fans enjoyed that "call it like he sees it" approach. He sounded more like a complaining fan than a "homer" announcer making excuses for the good guys.

Most announcers don't like handling any foul ball hit straight back. They certainly didn't try to catch something that fast without a glove, and many times the ball got back there so fast, they barely had time to react. Leaning out of the booth for a high one could land them first in the seats, and then in traction. Sometimes it was just better to duck and hide.

Caray figured he had at least a partial solution. He took a long handled fish net to the booth. It provided some security against a screaming line drive, and he didn't have to worry about leaning his portly body too far over the side of the booth. Although the logic was sound, it didn't seem likely that he would come close to picking up a souvenir, especially after impairing himself with a few Budweisers.

In 1972, Caray did occasional radio broadcast from the center field bleachers. The bleachers were bleachers in the true sense of the word. The cheapest seats in the house, they were nothing but backless benches located anywhere from 470 to over 500 feet from home plate. Their greatest advantages included the low price and the center field camera-type look at the pitch. Their primary disadvantage was the almost no chance for a fan to corral a home run ball because of the straightaway distance from home plate. In fact there was a 32-year stretch where no homers were hit into those bleachers, and only three had landed there after the bleachers were constructed in 1927.

On August 23, 1972, Caray picked up his gear, including his fishing net, and started for the bleachers. GM Roland Hemond was more than amused that Harry actually thought he would have any use for that net. Not only he was in those bleachers, he sat high up to get the best overall view of the game. It would take some kind of a clout for Caray to even get close to a home run.

In the seventh inning, Dick Allen faced Lindy McDaniel of the New York Yankees. Allen, already in later stages of a career season, sent a drive to center field. From the actions of Yankee outfielder Bobby Murcer, there was no doubt that the ball was leaving the park. He even had a second to rest by the 400-foot sign and get a real good look at another prodigious Dick Allen home run. But this was not just another home run, not even for Allen. Sox fan Mark Liptak sat in those bleachers not very far from Caray. He not only had a good look at the amazing home run, he also got an excellent view of the amazed expression on Mercer's face. According to Liptak, the ball was still climbing even as it cleared the fence in one of the deepest parts of Comiskey.

Caray was ready. Who knows? Maybe he came closer to snaring this drive than he did with any foul ball hit behind the plate. Leaning over the table set up in front of him, Caray looked like a fisherman reeling in a new catch. The drive was hit directly at him, but it didn't quite have the distance to give him a real good chance to catch it, net or no net.

A fan did get the home run, an oh-so-rare thing in the bleachers. Liptak said the fan showed the ball to Caray even though he didn't want to interrupt the broadcast. But Caray was happy the fan caught his attention and called the guy over. "He [Caray] interviewed the guy right in the middle of the play-by-play," Liptak said. "He asked the fan, 'How close did I come to getting that ball?' 'About five yards, Harry,' was the fan's reply."

Liptak said Caray then sent the fan on his way after congratulating him about his new souvenir. He then repeated the story to his audience so they could visualize a home run ball actually finding its way into the Comiskey Park bleachers.

Three more drives made it into the bleachers before the demolition of Comiskey. In the entire history of the park, only two White Sox players pulled off the feat. Richie Zisk did it in the unbelievable year of 1977. The other one, the one Harry Caray almost reeled it in with his net, was Allen's. And that is no fish story.

On a Clear Day You Can See Forever

There is no greater intangible than the weather.

In late December 1988, the Chicago Bears played the Philadelphia Eagles in a NFC playoff game that became known as the "Fog Bowl." When the game began on that late Sunday afternoon, the sky was bright and clear; it was a perfect day for football. At the half, the Bears had the lead, hoping for their third appearance in the NFC championship game in five years

To the surprise of all, the visibility disappeared during the second half. An early evening fog rolled in off Lake Michigan and almost completely engulfed Soldier Field. TV viewers truly watched the game in a fog, as they had to totally rely on audio play-by-play accounts to follow the action. The Bears won that game, but had no such luck in the NFC championship contest a week later under an artificially lit Solder Field in a late afternoon, early evening game. The winter sky, which had turned dark by the third quarter, remained very clear. Bear fans had a great view of a 28-3 Bears defeat.

Over 12 years earlier, the White Sox experienced a "fog bowl" of their own. Playing a night game against the Texas Rangers on May 31, 1976, Chicago got a break from Mother Nature. The result was a key hit in a win that would not have playoff ramifications but would delight those in attendance.

During the last week in May, Chicago got hit with monsoon-like storms. During this bad weather, Illinois high school baseball championships were played at Comiskey. The uncovered infield, which became more soaked than usual, forced left fielder Ralph Garr to take 30 steps in the batting cage just to find solid ground. Along with a wet field came a thick fog at a very opportune time.

Down 2-0, the Sox had the bases loaded and two out in the bottom of the first. Chet Lemon then hit what normally was a routine fly ball to left. Texas outfielder Tom Grieve came in and looked like he was going to camp under the ball. Suddenly, he stopped, and spread his arms out in frustration. Looking right up into the thick mist, Grieve had lost the ball in the fog.

It plopped down about thirty feet in front of him without even a bounce. It just sat there in the tall wet grass, hiding like an egg in an Easter egg hunt. From the first base side, it had been visible both in the air and on the ground. However, by the time anyone on the Rangers found the ball, Lemon was sliding into third with a triple and three RBIs. Sox fans wildly cheered their luck.

The umpiring crew met with both sides after the inning ended. Play would be stopped any time the umps ruled that the fog ruined visibility. On hearing this decision announced, Sox fans let out a good, long, loud boo. Hell, if it worked one time, why not another? Some of the fans sitting on the first base side imagined Bill Veeck on the roof with a huge fan, blowing the fog over the field when the White Sox were up. Baseball at Comiskey was fun once more.

The Sox won the game 9-4. Like the 1988 Bears, they were on a roll, winning 12 out of their last 15. Chicago stood a mere three games out of first in the Western Division. But also like the Bears, their fortunes faded and they ended up last.

Although last place is nothing to brag to your girlfriend about, the White Sox could at least say they hosted and won the first fog bowl in Chicago.

Short Pants Day

Bill Veeck, like him or not, was a man with ideas.

He could make some controversial decisions, such as trading away young talent for aging veterans in the early '60s or acquiring Claudell Washington in 1978. Yet the man never stopped trying to draw fans to the ball park with promotions or anything entertaining. The exploding scoreboard was his greatest idea. Fireworks add greatly to the excitement of a home run, and the exploding scoreboard became a large part of White Sox history.

On August 8, 1976, the baseball owner/showman tried another new idea. For the first time in Major League Baseball history, a team took the field in short pants. Had White Sox fans been asked what the team needed in 1976, they would not have mentioned exposed knees. In fact, for almost anyone, it would have been anything but that. But in the first game of a doubleheader against Kansas City, the White Sox followed the edict of their CEO. They took the field showing their wares in Bermuda shorts and white knee socks.

"You're the sweetest team we've seen yet," said huge and cuddly acting Royals first baseman John Mayberry. Mayberry also described the less then slender Sox relief pitcher Clay Carroll as having the look of "a pilgrim ready to shoot a wild turkey."

In addition, the Sox picked a cold day to dress warm. Even though it was August, the temperature never broke 80 and the Sox went out dressed for a day at the beach. No, the day wasn't really that cold, but it also wasn't a good day for the wind blowing up your skirt.

Despite the jeers and the catcalls from opposing players and fans, the Sox won the first game of the doubleheader 5-2. One would have to wonder if the Royals were embarrassed being beaten by a bunch of guys who looked like they were ready for their first day in grade school. If they were embarrassed, the Royals didn't show it when they won the second game. They also didn't show it when they clinched the Western Division title about six weeks later.

The shorts? The Sox didn't wear them in the second game and they were never seen again. John Mayberry was probably the only person who missed them.

Hurts So Bad You Have to Laugh

For the White Sox and their fans, it's not really that funny.

On October 8, 1983, the South Side Chicago ball club played the Baltimore Orioles in the fourth game of the American League Championship series. Down two games to one in a best-of-five match-up, Chicago had to win or go home. This game would actually be their best shot at a World Series from 1960 to 2003. Best shot or not, all that really remains now are memories of "what ifs" and the frustration of a great opportunity lost. So intense is the pain that fans are better off laughing than driving themselves insane rehashing the twisted events that conspired against their team.

For it isn't really funny that Jerry Dybzinksi made a crucial base running mistake that was completely out of character for him. And it wasn't really funny that Dybzinksi stood on third base after singling in the ninth representing the game's winning run and then died there as Tippy Martinez dropped a beautiful curve on the inside corner to Rudy Law on a full count to end the inning. And it wasn't funny at all that a guy with 41 regular season at-bats hits the game winning home run into the upper deck while one rooftop homer-hitting Sox slugger, Greg Luzinski, went 0 for 5; and another one, Ron Kittle, was too hurt to play. (Luzinski had a particularly bad day, never putting the ball in play. He was called out on strikes three times and fouled out twice.)

But laughing is better than basket weaving.

After taking their division by 20 games, the Sox psyche was at a season low entering game four. Mike Boddicker set a then playoff record of 14 strikeouts, shutting them out 4-0 in game two in Baltimore. In game three, in the first post-season game played in Chicago since Eisenhower was president, the Orioles trampled the Sox 11-1 in a bean ball, anger-filled contest. Winning Ugly had turned into losing ugly, making it feel like midnight had arrived for Cinderella.

Britt Burns started game four for Chicago. At one time, Burns was considered the best up and coming left-handed pitcher in the American League. In 1980 he won 15 in his first full season for a club that was awful. In the strike and injury shortened seasons of '81 and '82, Burns compiled a mark of 23-11. He remembers that his velocity dropped off in 1983, which may have been attributed to a late 1982 injury that he says was never fully diagnosed. Whatever the reason, he slumped during the Winning Ugly year, finishing at 10-11. He felt that game four was a chance to redeem himself for a disappointing 1983 regular season.

"On a couple occasions, Tony [La Russa, Sox manager] called me into his office," Burns recalls. "He told me I had been complacent, but did well when I felt challenged. He said I had it in me to succeed and had to tap into that more often."

Burns also felt he had not performed up to what LaMarr Hoyt, Richard Dotson, and Floyd Bannister had accomplished in 1983. Those three combined for 62 wins and were almost un-hittable during the last half of the season. He wanted to prove he belonged in their company. In addition, Burns wanted to prove he could pitch in a big game. Although there was tension and bad blood between the Sox and Baltimore spilling over from the brawling game the night before, Burns wasn't concerned with any after effects as he prepared to pitch the biggest game of his career.

"I had to be certain of what I was going to do at the moment," he says. "You can't let those things interfere." From his performance, it was fairly obvious that Britt Burns was focused.

Baltimore threatened throughout the game but couldn't score. The O's most serious threat came in the eighth when they loaded the bases with two out. Burns got out of that jam when he induced Dan Ford to pop out to Sox second baseman Julio Cruz. He then got the side out in order in the ninth with groundballs to third, short and second. He had given up but five hits in what should have been a complete game shutout.

Meanwhile, the Sox couldn't deliver a key hit. And when it did look like they would finally break through with at least one run, one of their most reliable role players made a base running gaffe that didn't make sense even after he explained it. (To Jerry Dybzinksi's credit, he never ran away from anyone asking just what in the hell was he doing that day.)

With one out, Vance Law on second and Jerry Dybzinski on first, Julio Cruz knocked a sharp single to left in between short and third. Not only was the ball hit hard, left fielder Gary Roenicke wasn't playing deep. Law barely made his turn at third when he put on the breaks, having no intention of trying to score. Dybzinksi continued on his way to the still occupied third base and was caught in a rundown. Hoping the Orioles would be distracted by Dybzinksi, Law scampered for home only to be cut down on a throw from Rich Dauer to Rick Dempsey. Law's attempt to run over the brick wall Dempsey was futile. The 45,477 Sox fans in attendance were stunned into a disbelieving silence.

Rudy Law hit next, with two outs. He sent a fly deep enough to left that would have scored anyone on third but was now the third out of the inning.

It looked like the Sox would go out meekly in the ninth when Mike Squires grounded out and Vance Law flew out. But then Jerry Dybzinksi atoned for his seventh inning miscue by singling. He went to third when Julio Cruz picked up his third single of the day. Cruz took second as left-handed Oriole pitcher Tippy Martinez was only concerned with hitter Rudy Law.

Law worked Martinez to a full count. Right-handed hitting Carlton Fisk was on deck. Martinez definitely didn't want to face Fisk, and loading the bases was also not a great option. Considering the situation, Law may have thought that Martinez had no choice but to throw a fastball. When Law took a third strike, fans who were unable to see the pitch had to wonder how he could not be swinging in that situation.

But in looking at the pitch, it was obvious why Law was fooled. Martinez threw a hook on the inside corner, at the knees. Even if the tied up looking Law had swung, it was doubtful he could have done anything with the pitch. Martinez just came through, winning a gamble that he was able to spot a breaking pitch in the strike zone on a full count.

Burns came out for the tenth and started out strong by getting John Shelby on a called third strike. Tito Landrum then stepped up and effectively ended the Sox season by hitting a solo home run into the first row of the left field upper deck, breaking the scoreless tie. Burns doesn't have any regrets about throwing the lightly regarded Landrum a fastball. Cal Ripken Jr., Eddie Murray, and Gary Roenicke (Sox killer, two RBI and three runs scored in game two) were next to hit. "Those guys get more fast balls," Burns says, referring to less dangerous hitters like Landrum.

He describes the pitch as a four-seam fastball that was in the strike zone. Throwing strikes is what a pitcher is supposed to do, he explained, even though a pitcher exposes himself to a hitter any time he does that, and he also said that Landrum "centered" the pitch well. "I couldn't have done anything different," he maintains, defending his decision to challenge Landrum.

According to now Sox radio announcer Ed Farmer, Cal Ripken saluted Burns when he was taken out of the game by standing on the Baltimore dugout steps and giving the Sox lefty a one man standing ovation. The ovation was deserved as Burns redeemed himself by pitching the game of his life in a pressure situation

Burns had come through, but October 8, 1993, was a dark, dreary and cold fall day. In a page one headline the next day the *Chicago Sun-Times* called it the "Ugliest Day of the Year," for different reasons. For the Sox and their fans, it was truly painful—but only when they laughed.

Angering the Gods of Old Comiskey

Baseball is not baseball without superstition and ritual.

On April 18, 1991, something occurred in Chicago that hadn't happened in three-quarters of a century: The city had a new baseball stadium. From the time the group headed by Jerry Reinsdorf and Eddie Einhorn purchased the Sox, they argued that the White Sox needed a new stadium if they were going truly compete as a major league franchise. The old park was falling apart, obsolete and rehabbing it was out of the question. Old Comiskey was grand, but it was more old than grand. The White Sox had to have a new place to play.

Many didn't want to see Old Comiskey go, but it was still an exciting day for baseball fans in Chicago. Not only did they have a new stadium, the Sox had gotten off to a great start by winning six of seven road games. After winning 94 the previous season, it appeared that they were going to contend for something big. Jack McDowell had already won his first two starts and was coming off a 17-win, 1990 season. Surely they would treat their fans to a great home opener against the Detroit Tigers.

Well, they fell a little short in that last regard. Maybe they had first day jitters. The White Sox laid their biggest home opening egg since a 12-0 pounding by Minnesota in 1970. By the bottom of the fourth inning, the Tigers were pulling some of their starters from the game. They could afford to with tough left-hander Frank Tanana on the mound and a 16-0 lead.

Detroit came up with six in the third inning and a whopping ten in the fourth. McDowell looked like some guy from the '70 squad. His relievers looked like they had the same sense of history. A comeback wasn't likely. The Sox offense got just seven singles for the day. Scoring was a fantasy from another dimension. The Tigers didn't score after their explosion in the fourth, but they didn't need any more runs. It turned out that their 16 tallies were a little overkill. Detroit won 16-0. "We just wanted to get the game over with," Don Pall says of game most Sox fans don't want to remember. Pall came in to pitch the eighth.

As with all games, good and bad, the 1991 home opener did end. Afterward, McDowell said he sat with a group of teammates, laughed a little and wondered aloud, "What was that all about?"

McDowell came to the conclusion that the new park opening with new player uniforms had tromped on tradition and "angered the Gods of Old Comiskey." So, McDowell says he, Scott Radinksy and Robin Ventura went out to second base before the next day's game. In a scene reminiscent of Disco Demolition, McDowell said they burned a uniform right there in the middle of the diamond, hoping the sacrifice would wipe away any curse that may have been cast on them or the new ballpark. According to McDowell, the sacrifice worked like a charm.

"The next day Rob Deer [Tiger right fielder] stumbled and let a line drive get past him," McDowell recalled, sure that Deer had suffered the same infliction that haunted the Sox the day before. McDowell was certain that there was no reason for Deer to stumble on the Lance Johnson double. The right field sun wasn't particularly bright, and there was no debris on the field. Deer wasn't known as a great outfielder, but McDowell maintained the sacrifice worked. The former Sox pitcher felt that the Gods of Old Comiskey were now at peace and supporting the White Sox.

Gods or no Gods, the Sox lost that game in 12 innings. They had to wait until the following day to win their first game at the new ballpark.

Regardless, the White Sox still had a historic season of sorts in 1991. They set a Sox attendance record of over 2.9 million and their tickets were being scalped in the streets again. They had a young pitcher who threw a no-hitter, and some developing players that showed a great deal of potential. Unfortunately they lost 12 out of 14 in late August, playing themselves right out of contention. Some other types of history would have to wait.

Arthur Allyn Jr. was the principal owner of the White Sox during the '60s. Allyn's team had three straight 90-plus-win seasons in the middle of the decade but could not make it to the World Series. (Courtesy of the Mark Fletcher Photo Collection.)

The White Sox had started the 1968 season with a losing streak, yet manager Eddie Stanky seems unconcerned. Here he suns himself in the left field seats as his team works out or appears to work out. (Courtesy of the Leo Bauby Photo Collection.)

The "Boston Massacre" of May 31, 1970: The scoreboard tells it all. (Courtesy of the Leo Bauby Photo Collection.)

John Allyn oversaw the 1970 disaster during his first full season as owner. His team lost 106 that year, including 12 doubleheader sweeps. Looked upon as a decent man, John Allyn helped to keep the White Sox in Chicago first by buying controlling interests from his brother in September 1969, and second by selling to Bill Veeck instead of Seattle interests in 1975. (Courtesy of the Gerry Bilek Photo Collection.)

Harry Caray is right at home in the booth. Caray is strongly identified with the Cubs but actually began his Chicago broadcasting career with the Sox. Leading "Take Me Out to the Ballgame" during the seventh inning stretch was a Veeck idea that Caray perfected. In the background is the fishing net that Caray used to almost land a Dick Allen 1972 homer hit into the center field bleachers. (Courtesy of the Gerry Bilek Photo Collection.)

The centerfield wall is seen as it appeared during the second Veeck administration during the late '70s. Harry Caray's approximate location on the day Dick Allen hit his bleacher shot in 1972 is to the right of the white hand railing. (Courtesy of the Leo Bauby Photo Collection.)

From the looks of these guys, it was easy to see why the short pants uniform died a quick death. (Courtesy of the Leo Bauby Photo Collection.)

The "Monster" scoreboard is seen as it looked in the early part of the 1962 season. It is still a great symbol of the franchise. (Courtesy of the Mark Fletcher Photo Collection.)

The scoreboard erupts in the summer of 1961, celebrating a Luis Aparicio home run. The fan smiling in the lower left-hand corner says it all. (Courtesy of the Mark Fletcher Photo Collection.)

Not everyone appreciated the new exploding scoreboard at Comiskey Park. Mocking the idea of celebrating White Sox home runs with fireworks, Yankee players hold up sparklers after New York third baseman Clete Boyer had hit a two-run homer on June 17, 1960. Meanwhile the scoreboard has never lost its popularity, even in the second Comiskey Park now called U.S. Cellular Field. (Courtesy of the Gerry Bilek Photo Collection.)

In 1970, the Cincinnati Reds led by Johnny Bench, Tony Perez, and Pete Rose, were labeled as the Big Red Machine as they rolled to a World Series. The White Sox, trying to be the Big White Machine, chug along here in catcher Ed Herrmann's car to a last place finish. (Courtesy of the Mark Fletcher Photo Collection.)

Two great baseball men pose during the spring of 1969. Luke Appling (left) and Don Gutteridge could not keep the Sox from losing during the late '60s.

Manager Paul Richards in 1976. 1976 was Richards' second tour of duty as Sox skipper. During the early '50s he led the memorable and winning "Go-Go" White Sox. 1976 wasn't so successful. The team lost 97 and finished last.(Mark Fletcher photo collection.)

Britt Burns finishes his windup. Burns pitched the game of his life during Game Four of the 1983 American League Championship Series, only to lose when the potent Sox offense came up with zilch as far as run support. Burns had wanted to prove himself in that game, and he did. It was too bad his whole career didn't fulfill the promise showed when he came up to the Sox for good in 1980. (Photo by Mark Fletcher.)

SIX

The South Side
Hit Men

A Richie Zisk story from 1977 went that the White Sox right fielder kept a ball in his locker as a souvenir. It wasn't from a home run he had hit, but he had ripped into it so hard that the stitching had unraveled. This may be just an urban tale, but most White Sox fans with memories of 1977 will believe it. Literally or figuratively, the White Sox just knocked the stitching off the ball that year. Like so many Sox teams, the 1977 South Side Hit Men didn't make it to the World Series. Unlike so many Sox teams of the 1970s, they provided life-long memories.

A New Tradition . . . At Least for Three Days Anyway
History repeats itself, sometimes.

The White Sox had a tradition in the early to mid-'60s. They'd be in second place or in near contention when the first place team, usually the New York Yankees, came into town. The Yankees would then demolish the Sox, and any hopes for a Chicago World Series quickly faded. In the first days of July 1977, the first place Minnesota Twins came in for single games on Friday and Saturday and a doubleheader the day before the fourth of July. Even though the Twins had a one game lead on the Sox at the time of their arrival, by the time the series was over, they were three games behind the Sox and continued to recede as a major player in the Western Division race. During that weekend, Chicago baseball history did not repeat itself.

There were likely and unlikely Sox heroes in the series. They had good pitching and key home runs. Drawing nearly 100,000 for the three dates, the team and fans had formed an unbreakable bond. Fans of the '70s vintage remember this series as one of the best played at Comiskey during the decade.

Richie Zisk, one of the most popular players of the South Side Hit Men, was overwhelmed by the outpouring of fan affection in 1977. He responded in game one with two home runs as he knocked in all five Sox runs in a 5-2 Sox win. Paced by a complete game performance by Chris Knapp, the White Sox inched themselves up into first place. It was by mere percentage points, but they were back on top of the Western Division.

"Oh, For the Long Lone," proclaimed the banner commonly held in the left field seats in 1977. In game two, first baseman Jim Spencer provided two long ones—a grand slam and a three-run shot in the eighth that capped a seven-run inning. Spencer knocked in eight for the game, one of two times he performed that feat in 1977. The final was 13-8; a typical whooping the Sox offense handed out that season.

Doubleheaders were not always kind to the White Sox in the late '60s and throughout the '70s. But in these two Sunday games, they looked like they were made to play doubleheaders.

Wilbur Wood was not himself as he took the mound in game one, still trying to regain his form after the injury inflected by the Ron LeFlore line drive in May 1976. Wood took a 1-2 record into this game. In his prime, he was capable of picking up three decisions in a week, rather than by nearly mid-season.

But in this contest, he looked like the Cy Young Award contender he had been in 1971 and '72. He gave up three little hits to the hard-hitting Twins, all singles. After the first, no Twin advanced past second. The White Sox didn't use the long ball in this game, but they won convincingly enough 6-0.

Game two instigated what was to become a controversial part of the 1977 season: The fan curtain call. Jim Spencer hit his third home run in two days, a two-run shot that helped the Sox out to a 4-0 lead in the first. Spencer stood right outside the dugout and tipped his hat to the nearly 34,000 fans who had become totally infatuated with their team.

In the fourth, two unlikely sluggers came through for the Sox. Catcher Jim Essian and shortstop Alan Bannister hit back-to-back home runs in another four-run Sox rally. They also each came out for a curtain call, leaving opposition teams with the impression that they were being shown up by the Sox.

Sox fan Mark Liptak, who attended the doubleheader, looks at the situation differently, saying there was no intention to do anything insulting to visiting ball clubs." The fans were cheering so loud that there was no choice. The game just couldn't continue. The fans demanded it [that the player come out and acknowledge the ovation.]."

In 2003, Liptak's interviewed Sox third baseman and South Side hitman Eric Soherholm for the whitesoxinteractive website, and Soderholm said he loved the fans for the curtain calls but was not all that crazy about the whole concept. "When the curtain calls started I was uncomfortable with that," Soderholm told Liptak. "Several players were. It could be misunderstood by the other team that we were trying to show them up, talking trash and that kind of stuff. I understood where the fans were coming from in all this. They were happy, excited and the support was wonderful. They were producing a lot of positive energy and that helped us. After a while, you felt obligated to come out and respond to them, even if you weren't comfortable."

With Chicago leading 8-2 after the Bannister and Essian home runs, the Twins didn't give up, but their comeback fell short. The Sox won 10-8, completing a four-game sweep. Reliever Larrin LaGrow struck out the dangerous Larry Hisle to end the game and the crowd erupted once again. "They were chanting we're number one," said Liptak. "It was great after the Nineteen Seventy-Three, Seventy-Six seasons that were just lost years."

First place after sweeping another contender; it just didn't happen to the White Sox often. But the 1977 squad was not just any Sox team. It was a time when baseball rocked on the south side of Chicago. It even looked like the White Sox would rock themselves right into the World Series.

One of the Last Great Days of the Decade
The South Side Hit Men had been on a roll.

The Chicago White Sox and their fans didn't know it at the time, but July 31, 1977, was the last high point of the 1970s. Only a few dramatic games in the earlier part of that decade could compete with the first game of that doubleheader with the Kansas City Royals. Nothing that happened during the remaining part of the '70s came close; unless you want to count the night the stadium was almost burnt to the ground.

By 1976 the Royals supplanted the Oakland A's as the class team of the Western Division. Their everyday lineup boasted the likes of George Brett, Hal McRae, Al Cowens, John Mayberry and Amos Otis. They won their first division crown in 1976 and were definitely the team to beat in the division in 1977.

The Royals came into Chicago the last weekend of July to face the first place White Sox. The Sox were putting the finishes on what would turn out to be their best month in the whole decade, going 22-6. They had no real defense, speed only in spots and no dominating starting pitcher. They were a ragtag bunch of players that other teams didn't want. But they could hit, and to say they could hit didn't really come close to describing the offensive fire power of the club.

Although the White Sox had home run champions in Dick Allen and Bill Melton during the start of the decade, they still didn't have what could be considered an overall great hitting line up. The World Series squad of 1959 was the typical scratching and clawing for runs Sox team. Many White Sox fans longed to see the excitement that only a power hitting team could provide.

And the 1977 team did just that and in a manner that few Sox fans anticipated or expected that year. The South Side Hit Men, as the 1977 Sox would be known, just hit the hell out of the ball. Richie Zisk, acquired from Pittsburgh, had a career year that included a homer against New York on the left field Comiskey Park roof. Oscar Gamble, obtained from the Yankees, became the first left-handed hitter in Sox history to hit 30 home runs in a season. Eric Soderholm won the Comeback Player of the Year Award by hitting 25 homers after missing the entire 1976 season due to a knee injury. First baseman Jim Spencer had two eight RBI days. No opposing pitcher was safe from the Sox offensive onslaught, and their fans loved them for it.

In the first game of the doubleheader against the Royals, the Sox uncharacatesically picked up a mere six hits in a game that went ten innings. Yet that game was just another demonstration of the Sox power and clutch hitting that made them one of the most memorable Sox teams during the last half of the century.

The hitting star of this game was Chet Lemon. Playing in his second full season, Lemon was just starting to come into his own as a major league hitter. He homered in the sixth inning off of Marty Pattin to tie the game at one. In the bottom of the tenth, he tied the game once more with a home run. Facing the tough side-armed throwing Doug Bird, Lemon hit a two-run shot into about the fifth row of lower deck. It was just another multi-homer game by a Sox player that year, and the crowd of 50,412 roared their approval.

One out later Ralph Garr singled home the winning run, and Comiskey Park went wild one more time. The Sox had started the month by vanquishing the Minnesota Twins, and now, after winning the first three games of a four game set, looked like they were going to dethrone the defending division champion Royals. It seemed like decades since the Dick Allen MVP year. Could this be it?

Eric Soderholm remembers this series as the high point of the emotional 1977 campaign. He especially remembers the feeling of circling the bases the day before when his three-run homer in the seventh put the Sox ahead for good in a game they won 6-4. "The place just went nuts," Soderholm recalls. "I have never felt such a roar. I remember touching second and feeling all that energy."

But was this it? Were the White Sox finally on their way to a championship of some kind? Well, no. Kansas City won the second game of that doubleheader 8-4 and more importantly gained a psychological edge on the White Sox. After hitting a seventh inning homer, Kansas City outfielder Hal McRae slowly trotted around the bases, tipping his hat to the crowd as he went by. McRae thought the fan curtain calls had gone way too far and later said he wanted the Sox and their fans to see how stupid they looked.

"He was making a mockery of what we were doing," Soderholm says.

The White Sox traveled to Kansas City the next weekend and were swept in a three game series.In the first game they were pounded 12-2 as Royal players continued to mock them by tipping their hats to the fans. More importantly the Royals continued on a winning rampage that Soderholm feels was partially motivated by the curtain calls at Comiskey. Kansas City took the division by a comfortable 10-game margin over second place Texas and 12 ahead of the third place Sox.

But the first game on July 31, 1977, still ranks as a high mark during the last four decades. The South Side Hit Men, with their 22-6 record that month, averaged over six runs a game. Even the 1959 pennant winners didn't have a month that good. Since then only the 1983 Winning Ugly team matched that winning percentage, going 22-6 in September when they ran away and hid with that year's division race.

July 31, 1977: White Sox fans could only look back and wish the regular season could have ended on that day.

Last Day of the South Side Hit Men

It was truly the last day of the season.

The White Sox had long since been eliminated, not that there had been real suspense in the last month of the season anyway. Not only did White Sox fans say good-bye to the team for the season, they knew that at least a few of the players would be gone for good. No one expected both Richie Zisk and Oscar Gamble to return because they were eligible for free agency, and most expected both to leave. Big first baseman Jim Spencer would eventually be sent away in what was essentially a cash deal. The days of the South Side Hit Men were numbered and, sadly, short lived.

The White Sox began the season in Toronto providing the opposition for the expansion Blue Jays in the middle of a snowstorm. They embarrassed themselves by giving Toronto its first ever franchise victory, losing 9-5. To end 1977, the Sox played the other expansion team of that year, the Seattle Mariners. The cold, dark, and wet October afternoon was similar to the Toronto opener. The Sox again looked uninspired in losing 3-2, not that the result mattered. The Sox had a lock on third place whether they won or lost that day.

But this wasn't like so many other last games of the season when the Sox finished another year with no championship. The 1977 team accomplished a great deal, developing a lasting love affair with the fans that is simply unforgettable.

Number one accomplishment: They won 90. It was the only time they reached the 90-win plateau in the '70s and the first time since 1965. No baseball expert picked them for anything near 90 wins and most thought last place was a real possibility, even with the expansion Seattle Mariners in the same division.

Number two accomplishment: They set a then White Sox attendance record of 1,657,135 which inched past the old mark set in 1960. The 1960 team had the benefit of following the pennant winners of the season before. The Sox had finished last in 1976. They fell 7,858 short of the Chicago baseball record belonging to the doomed 1969 Cubs.

Number three accomplishment: They formed a great emotional connection with the fans. On hitting his 25^{t}h home run in the fifth inning in that last game, Eric Soderholm came out of the dugout for one more curtain call. Controversial or not, it was the last game of the season and he saluted the fans more than they saluted him. The South Side Hit Men received a standing ovation when they took the field for the last time in the ninth. Coming off the field, they received another one.

"I played for the Indians when we drew two million in one year," Sox manager Bob Lemon said. "And it was nothing like this. Never seen a summer like this. Between the Cubs and us, if you weren't talking baseball, you weren't talking."

Once the game ended and the season sadly ended also, fans didn't want to leave Comiskey. They stayed and cheered their team and owner Bill Veeck cheered them from his press box. The only thing that was truly missing was a trip to the post season, but one never would have known it from the happiness of the day. But then again, the fans had plenty to be happy about. The team hit 192 homers, setting a new team record. They were in first place from July 1 to August 12. They were a bunch of unwanted guys who had career years and revived a franchise that had been on death's door for two bleak seasons.

The year 1977: If they could only bottle it and mix in a World Championship, everybody would be rich.

It's Opening Day, 1977, and the Chicago White Sox, led by manager Bob Lemon (far right) are a motley, but beloved crew. (Courtesy of the Leo Bauby Photo Collection.)

In his playing days, Bob Lemon was a pitcher who won 207 games, and played for Bill Veeck's World Champion Cleveland Indians in 1948. Lemon thought the excitement in Chicago that summer matched the excitement in Cleveland. He left the Sox in mid-1978 and guided the Yankees to a World Championship that year. (Courtesy of the Gerry Bilek Photo Collection.)

Chet Lemon is pictured in his early years with the Sox. Lemon had the luck of hitting a routine fly ball in the middle of a fog at Comiskey Park one night in 1976. The thick mist turned the usual inning ending out into a three run triple. More importantly, the talented center fielder was a large part of the South Side Hit Men in 1977. He hit two home runs in one of the biggest wins of the decade on July 31, 1977. He eventually was traded to Detroit where he played on the World Champion Tigers in 1984.(Gerry Bilek photo collection.)

Alan Bannister, shortstop for the 1977 club, and future Cub manager Jim Essian hit back-to-back homers to help finish off a four-game sweep of the Minnesota Twins in early July. Bannister had a bad arm, however, and he made 40 errors that year, many of them of the throwing variety. (Courtesy of the Gerry Bilek Photo Collection.)

Oscar Gamble gets ready to take some BP during his career year 1977. Gamble was the first left-handed hitter to swat 30 homers in a season for the White Sox. Hitting from a slight crouch, Gamble golfed pitches into the upper deck. He left the Sox for San Diego, and like Richie Zisk, who left for Texas, Gamble would not enjoy the type of year he had in 1977. (Courtesy of the Gerry Bilek photo collection)

Oscar Gamble rounds third and is heading for home. A large crowd watches. (Courtesy of the Leo Bauby Photo Collection.)

Jim Spencer crosses home plate after hitting homer on Opening Day, 1976. Spencer was a large part of the South Side Hit Men, providing both power and excellent defensive work at first. (Courtesy of the Leo Bauby Photo Collection.)

Eric Soderholm was one of the great stories of the 1977 South Side Hit Men. Missing the 1976 season because of an off the field knee injury, Soderholm belted 25 homers, a career best. He hit a key home run in the four game series at the end of July against Kansas City. The series ended up being the high point of the season—and of the decade. (Courtesy of the Mark Fletcher Photo Collection.)

Richie Zisk is being greeted at the plate—a common occurrence in 1977—by Ralph Garr (left) and another Sox player. The White Sox scored runs in bunches in that year. (Courtesy of the Mark Fletcher Photo Collection.)

Richie Zisk waits on deck. Zisk hit 30 home runs and knocked in 101 in 1977. (Courtesy of the Leo Bauby Photo Collection.)

Bill Veeck is pictured one year after the South Side Hit Men. He couldn't recreate that magic, and many long seasons were ahead. (Courtesy of the Gerry Bilek Photo Collection.)

SEVEN

In a Class
All by Themselves

Some games or memories can't be lumped into any one category. This chapter recalls some of the truly unique experiences at both Comiskey Parks. As always with historic White Sox events, these memories convey a mixture of exhilaration, elation, tears, disappointment, and humor. It's baseball on the South Side of Chicago, and that just about says it all.

A Rare World Series Memory
The Fall Classic had evaded the Sox for decades.

The back cover photo to this book shows a crowd of people standing outside Comiskey Park waiting to buy tickets for a game. On the surface, this is not an extraordinary event by any means. In fact, on some other occasions, especially opening days, you might find more people mulling around outside the ballpark.

Yet, this photo is a truly extraordinary image. The date was October 1, 1959. The Chicago White Sox were hosting the Los Angeles Dodgers in the first game of the World Series. The fans in the photo were hoping to get standing-room tickets for the first White Sox post-season appearance in 40 years.

Comiskey was approaching its 50th birthday and still had not been painted the modern looking white. Fittingly, its dark appearance gave it that throw back feeling of the team's last World Series appearance, in 1919. The 1919 Series was one of the most infamous of all baseball history, but it also reminded Sox fans of how great the team could have been.

Ella Lackovic is now 83 years old and has had Chicago White Sox season tickets for 54 years. She has vivid memories of how it felt to attend a World Series game. "The atmosphere was jumping," she remembers. "I had a lot of dignitaries sitting around me. The only time they came was for the World Series. At least that was the only time I saw them."

Two celebrities sitting by her were entertainer Danny Thomas and *Chicago Sun-Times* columnist Irv Kupicent. Presently, Lackovic is an active member of the Windy City Sox Fans, an organization that helps raise funds for Children's Memorial Hospital and Major League Baseball Cancer Charities. "At least I can say I have been to a World Series game," Lackovic says. "I hope I go to another in my lifetime."

The '50s has to be considered one of the greatest decades in the history of the White Sox. After a miserable 60-win start in 1950, the Sox never finished worse than third for the remainder of the decade. (This represents a considerable feat in the old eight team-divisional set up.) Known as the "Go-Go Sox" during the '50s, the White Sox built their success around strong pitching, speed and a good defense. But recognizing that a team should not live on defense alone, the White Sox made a late season trade and picked up the power hitting Ted Kluszewski on August 25.

Kluszewski represented the opposite of the White Sox image and identity. Playing on a team with guys like "Little Looie" and "Little Nel," the 6-foot-2, 245-pound first baseman known as

"Big Klu" wore sleeveless jerseys to accommodate his massive forearms and bulging bicepts. He had led the National League in homers with 49 in 1954. No White Sox player equaled that number until Albert Belle in 1998.

Acquiring Kluszewski made sense. Although White Sox had to claw for runs, they were indeed very successful in the '50s. All they had to show for it, however, were some nice records and a continued frustration at watching the Yankees go the World Series, season after season. And if you were still concerned about defense, Big Klu was more than an adequate first baseman, leading National League first basemen in fielding for five straight seasons during the early and mid-50s.

In last month of the 1959 regular season, Kluszewski hit just two homers in 101 official at-bats. In the first game of the 1959 World Series, however, Kluszweski proved his addition was just the move the Sox needed to make.

"What really picked us up was when we got Big Klu," outfielder Al Smith said. "There wasn't nobody hittin' the long ball in our lineup other than Lollar and myself. He added some punch to the lineup."

In the first inning, Kluszewski drove in Nelson Fox with a single to right. He did his job, but the Sox didn't get the big guy to hit singles. In his next two at-bats, Big Klu would add the punch Al Smith had been talking about.

With center fielder Jim Landis on first in the third inning, Kluszewski gave the Sox what they had hoped for in a power hitter. Landis took off on a hit and run. Kluszewksi hit it all right. His drive went down the right field line and into the first row. The two-run homer gave the Sox a 5-0 lead.

Kluszeswki wasn't done. Landis was on base again in the fifth and the big guy delivered one more time. His second two-run homer knocked off the upper deck railing in right. The White Sox lead ballooned to 11-0 as Kluszewski delivered with three straight hits and five RBIs. There was no suspense left, at least not in this game.

Home run power: The White Sox hadn't much of it during 1959 and throughout franchise history. After the 11-0 shellacking of the National League champions, many naïve fans dreamed of a sweep and a world championship. It was all an illusion. The Sox only surpassed their Game One total by one run combined during the last five games, four of which they lost. The Dodgers, who had so much trouble with the Yankees in past World Series, had very little trouble with the White Sox.

Kluszewski hit a three-run homer in Game Six, but it did little to help his club. Los Angeles won that game 9-3 and took the series despite the fact that Big Klu had ten RBIs, still a record for a six-game World Series.

The 1959 Chicago White Sox still hold a unique position in team history. At this writing, that squad remains the only Sox club since 1919 to win the American League pennant. The 11-0 win powered by Kluszewski's two homers also remains the only home win for the Sox in post-season play since the 1919 scandal threw the team into a 40-year funk.

Where's a Scalper When You Need Him?

Could you imagine an overflowing Comiskey Park?

During the late '60s and on many, many days during the early '70s, getting a White Sox ticket wasn't all that difficult. A fan just had to show up on game day, saunter up to a ticket window—any ticket window—and tell the guy there where he or she wanted to sit. More often than not a fan didn't have to worry about sitting behind a pole, a problem some encountered during some Sox-Yankees series just a few years before.

Even as the team showed some life and rebirth in the early '70s, attendance was still a problem. The club had some big crowds like the 44,250 for the home opener in 1971, and the 51,904 who came for Bat Day 1972. However, getting a Sox ticket for Bat Day 1973 was a far different story, because even some who had tickets didn't see the game in person.

No one could have possibly known it back then, but May 20, 1973, was going to be the high point for the Chicago White Sox during the '70s until the South Side Hit Men came along four years later. On that brisk but very bright Sunday spring afternoon, it finally looked like the Sox had truly found themselves as a franchise. No more losing, no more seas of empty seats, no more self-doubts about a seemingly shrinking fan base.

Yes, the Bat Day promotion was partially responsible for the turnout. Comiskey Park was normally filled on bat day. But on May 20, 1973, it was different, as different it was ever could be. People were everywhere. They stood everywhere including on the scoreboard catwalk, sat in aisles, and even sat on the scoreboard. The park was so crowded that over 2,000 ticket holders had to get refunds because there just wasn't any room for them. Sox catcher Ed Herrmann was thrilled with the crowd but wondered where everyone would go if there was a fire.

The announced paid attendance for the game was 55,555. With the over 2,000 refunds that meant almost 58,000 people showed up on one day for a White Sox doubleheader. Some (like Bill Veeck) didn't believe the 55,555 could fit into Comiskey even with a crow bar. And all those fives? Yet, even if that number was inflated, it could not have been so by much. There just wasn't any room to move.

The Sox responded, at least in the first game. It was somewhat fitting that Carlos May and Bill Melton had good days. After the team fell off the face of earth in 1968, May and Melton were looked upon as the main young guys to revive the franchise. In game one, they were a combined four for eight, with two homers and seven runs batted in. Melton homered into the lower deck off ex-Cub and 1969 north side alumni Bill Hands in the first. May clubbed a three-run homer off of Dave Goltz in the fourth to effectively put the game out of reach.

The Sox knocked out 13 hits en route to a 9-3 win. Wilbur Wood won his 10th game going all the way. (Yes, 10th win. The Sox had played only 34 games up to that point, and Wood was already involved in 13 decisions.) They led the Western Division and had the second best overall record in the majors at that point. With their coming to within $5^1/_2$ games of first the previous year, it appeared that the Sox had finally gelled and were ready to do something truly special for the fans of Chicago.

There was only one small drawback to the day. For the second straight Bat Day and the huge crowd that came with it, Dick Allen was a non-starter for game two. This time there was no dramatic ninth inning appearance. Allen did pinch-hit, but it was in the fourth inning and he popped out to Rod Carew. The game was scoreless when Allen came in, but he was done for the day. He sat and watched his team go down to a 3-0 defeat.

A few days later, center fielder Ken Henderson would badly injure his knee on a play at the plate. Dick Allen would miss the last two months of the season with a leg injury of his own. The season, the decade, except for the excitement of 1977, was over.

Still, May 20, 1973, will stand out as a proud moment in team history. They were in first place, their fans were back, and their future looked bright. It was a great day to be a Sox fan, even for the over 2,000 that had to go home because there was no room at the inn.

Disco Demolition, a Name and Memory in Itself
It was a promotion that literally blew up in the face of the White Sox organization.

Even the most casual of baseball fan needs no explanation when the words Disco Demolition are used. Immediate images, mostly fires and general mayhem, come to mind. The event has haunted the White Sox as a franchise and Mike Veeck as a person for a quarter of a century now.

"It wasn't that bad. Dad was not at fault."

The above quotation comes from Mike Veeck in a brief note sent to this author. Bill Veeck might not have been technically at fault; though it is hard to believe that things weren't "that bad." Moreover, any time people talk about the Sox in historic terms Disco Demolition always comes up. Any time Mike Veeck is in the news, even though he has taken on numerous challenges since leaving the Sox, the Disco Demolition fiasco is forever tied to his name.

101

Veeck has since professed that the promotion was really too successful for its own good. In July 1979, the White Sox stunk, and attendance was again on decline. "Disco Demolition" brought out a near capacity crowd of 47,795 with even more people on the outside unable to get in. In essence, they were all dressed up with nowhere to go.

During the late 1970s there wasn't a word strong enough to describe rock and roll fans' revulsion to the success of disco music. "Saturday Night Fever," a movie about some New York guy who was only happy when on the disco dance floor, was a blockbuster hit, and its accompanying soundtrack sold millions. Discos competed with sporting events as fun night time activities. The Beatles, the Stones and the Who began taking a back seat to the Bee Gees and Donna Summer.

To pick up on the strong backlash to this music trend, the White Sox teamed up with radio disc jockeys Steve Dahl and Garry Meier to have a demolition of disco records between games of a Sox-Tigers doubleheader on July 12, 1979. It had to sound like a great idea. Dahl and Meier were just beginning to attract a strong fan base of their own, and the Sox needed a good crowd at Comiskey.

The concept was simple: With 98 cents and a disco record, a fan could gain admission into the park. (98.5 was the frequency of Dahl's WDAI-FM station.) The records would then be blown up between games in the name of rock and roll. Anti-disco fans would vent, the Sox would have their big crowd, and everybody would be happy.

Sox fan Jim Riordan lived at 36th and Parnell, two blocks from the park on. Shortly before the doubleheader, the then nine-year-old Riordan was throwing a rubber ball against his apartment building. He got a good look of the some the "fans" that made their way to the park.

"They weren't the prototypical fans that I usually saw," Riordan wrote in an e-mail account. "I noticed a lot of stoner looking guys getting out of their cars and I saw one particular guy come out with a stack of about twenty albums, Donna Summer being the one on the top. I then realized that that night was Disco Demolition."

Donn Pall was a teenage White Sox fan in 1979. The Evergreen Park native realized a boyhood dream by working as a relief pitcher for his favorite team from 1988 to '93. Pall sat in the stands for the scheduled doubleheader wanting to see some baseball. What he saw was chaos. He concurred with Riordan that this was not a typical baseball crowd. "A cloud of marijuana smoke hung over the stadium," Pall recalls. "It looked like a Grateful Dead concert. They couldn't have cared less about the game."

Pall saw one "fan" shimmy his way down the right field foul pole to the field. In 1979, the pole had a screen attached making the descent easier. He also saw people with cuts on their faces from flying LPs. (No cds back then.) He saw fires and people trying to climb over the outside walls attempting to get in for the destruction.

"When all hell broke loose," said Riordan who watched everything on Channel 44, "my parents decried the youth of today. I, on the other hand, was merely fascinated that mayhem was taking place within a block or two of my house."

"It was totally crazy," Pall said in a simple description that made him sound like a contemporary of Riordan's parents. "They wouldn't leave the field," he added, saying that appeals from Bill Veeck and Harry Caray were totally ignored.

According to Pall, the biggest problem with the crowd was that few of them were baseball fans. The fact that the destruction eventually forced the White Sox to forfeit the second game meant nothing to them. "The Sox couldn't afford to lose," Pall recalls, describing the plight of the team that year.

But lose they did, and not only the second game of the doubleheader that would really not mean much in the lackluster season. The franchise was embarrassed especially with pictures of out of control rock and roll fans and of Comiskey Park looking like the burning of American cities of the Sixties spread all over the country. Bill Veeck again came under fire for caring more about his promotions than the product he put on the field. Even his most ardent Chicago supporters didn't back him during this franchise crisis.

102

"The next day at day camp," Riordan recalls, "the counselors told the kids they could not wear any anti-Disco or Insane Coho Lips T-shirts anymore. A few kids had to go home and change. So while I was not there, I still have a vivid recollection of some of the things that happened that night. And I wasn't even arrested."

That is something for which to be grateful. Sharing a jail cell with someone from the anti-Disco crowd was no place for a nine year-old.

Last Day at Old Comiskey

Old Comiskey Park stood for 80 years.

The old stadium had been home to Luke Appling, Shoeless Joe Jackson, the "Go-Go Sox," the South Side Hit Men and Winning Ugly. For many the passing of the old park was very painful even with the argument that the old park was no longer structurally safe. The Seattle Mariners was Comiskey's last venue on September 30, 1990, and 42,849 came out on that Sunday afternoon to say farewell to the park but not to the baseball history the park symbolized.

It was somewhat fitting that the 1990 club played the last game at the old stadium. The 1990 Sox were a throw back to the old fashioned Sox teams. Devoid of superstars, the 1990 Sox played small ball to score runs, depended on fundamentals, and won by unspectacular scores. Their leading home run hitter was an old guy named Carlton Fisk who belted a grand total of 18. No pitcher won 20 games. There was no real base stealing threat. They didn't do anything real exciting. They just won ball games.

"I think we had a bunch of midgets," Ozzie Guillen, now Sox manager, told the author. "We were the smurf team. I think I was the biggest guy on the field besides Frank. (Thomas)"

Donn Pall was a relief pitcher for the 1990 club. A Sox fan all his life, the old stadium meant a great deal to Pall. He said the demise of the old place was lost on many of his teammates who had no appreciation of the park's history. But Pall felt the history and wanted to remember. "I walked around the place," he said, thinking of the park's last days. "I sat in different seats, behind poles and remembered how it was like to see things."

Gerry Bilek, a Sox season ticket holder, attended the September 30 contest. He climbed to the upper deck behind the plate in seats that he considered some of the best in the house. "I watched Nancy Faust (Sox organ player) play in her booth," Bilek says. "Everyone was snapping Nancy's photo, asking her how she felt, her favorite songs, memories and players. She was very accommodating to the fans smiling and signing baseballs. Then I saw a tear on Nancy's cheek, followed by many more. She cried a bit and then composed herself and kept playing like the professional she is. I know that I, as well as the others around her, felt a little bit of what she was experiencing."

The Sox won 2-1 that day. It was type of win that was so much like the team that year, so much like the 1967 team that barely missed the World Series and the team of 1959, the last team to make it to the big time. They won because of a bad hop triple, they won because they didn't make any big mistakes, and they won with both good starting and relief pitching (Jack McDowell's 17th win and Bobby Thigpen's major league record-setting 57th save). They won in the White Sox historical way that could only invoke decades of memories.

The last out came on a ground ball off the bat of Harold Reynolds. The ball skidded out to second baseman Scott Fletcher. Fletcher's throw to first baseman Steve Lyons was in plenty of time. The Mariners had the tying run on first. It died there.

Fans held up signs that read, "Good-Bye, Old Friend," "Thanks for the Memories," and "Years From Now, We'll Say We Wuz Here." Tears flowed everywhere. Maybe chunks of cement were falling off of the place; maybe Comiskey was just too old. Maybe it was just an inevitability that the place had to go. But too much had happened there and saying good-bye was an emotional experience. In fact, there were some fans that sneaked into the place during its demolition to sit in it one more time, just to remember.

The New Comiskey, now called U.S. Cellular Field, opened the next year and drew almost three million in its inaugural season. It was not open long before it was criticized for a steep upper deck, a sterile atmosphere and an unstately appearance. The new park has gone through renovations and only time will tell if fans will ever love it as much as the older park. One thing is certain: The original Comiskey Park, known for its stately arching windows, stunning beauty at night and decades of memorable games, will not be forgotten.

Cross Town Sweep
There is something special about Cubs-Sox inter-league play.
The crowds are much larger, at least on the South Side. The atmosphere is more charged. The games mean no more than any other championship game, and actually, they mean a little less. However, big time Chicago baseball bragging rights are involved in these contests. No fan on either side of the Chicago baseball ledger wants to see his team get whooped in these encounters especially when, at this writing, there has been no World Series in the Windy City since 1959. Winning these games was almost like winning the World Series.

Neither side wants to admit how important these games are to them. But no matter what any White Sox player says, it is more than obvious from their intensity—their eagerness (such as Ray Durham practically running up to the plate to hit on one occasion) and their strong and emotional facial expressions—that winning these games is extremely important to them.

"We wanted to show that there is more than one team in this town," White Sox shortstop Jose Valentin said when interviewed at SoxFest 2004. Valentin is the shortstop whose has thrown balls into the seats behind first giving fans another excuse to call the beer vendor. Mind-boggling defensive lapses or not, Sox fans still admire Valentin's spirit, leadership and power from the left side of the plate. They loved his mocking of Sammy Sosa when Valentin did his own kiss blowing routine after clubbing a home run at Wrigley. (Valentin blew kisses at the crowd after crossing home plate, and, when discovering he knew the camera was on him in the dugout, pumped his chest and blew kisses again. A better imitation of Sammy Sosa has not been done.)

Valentin's feelings are somewhat hurt by the Cub mania in Chicago. When he hears of any public opinion sampling where it seems everyone is a Cub fan, it makes Valentin "sad."

Obviously the Cubs don't go into these games willing or wanting to lose. It is also obvious that they and their fans want the bragging rights as well. But it is also obvious that winning these games means more to the Sox since they are looked upon as second-class citizens in the second city. And what transpired in 1999 is remembered by Sox fans with such glee that it brings a joyful tear to the eye.

The Sox swept the Cubs, three games to none—at Wrigley.

There's nothing like winning a series on the road and it is even sweeter when the road sweep is won without leaving home. The 1999 three game sweep by the Sox at Wrigley in the first week of June will always rank as one of the great memories in White Sox lore.

1999 was not supposed to be a good year for the Sox. In the middle of a rebuilding program, they began the season with a mere 26,243 at their home opener. Playing on a blustery and cold day in some of the worst weather for a home Sox game, the South Siders lost to the small market Kansas City Royals 10-5. Chicago committed five errors in a game that didn't spring hope eternal.

Meanwhile the Cubs were coming off their 1998 "Wild Card Championship" season that featured Sammy Sosa hitting an incredible 66 home runs. More importantly, the Cubbies came into the series with a 32-24 mark, only two games behind the Central leading Houston Astros. The Sox record wasn't all that bad—2 games under .500 with a young team—but it looked like the series was an opportunity for the Cubs to show up the Sox while making a real run at their division.

Surpirse, surprise.

Early June is known to be wet in Chicago and rain helped the Sox win the first game of the series. The South Siders were able to pick up a 5-3 victory in a shortened $5\frac{1}{2}$ inning game. Sox fans happily sang the "Good-Bye Song" as they left rain soaked Wrigley. Some Cub fans challenged them to take it outside.

Game two was all White Sox. Young left hander Mike Sirotka threw $7^2/_3$ scoreless innings and the Sox coasted to 8-2 victory. Cub fans were ready for massive group therapy.

The July 31, 1997 "White Flag Trade," which sent three veteran Sox players to the San Francisco Giants for six unknown players, caused a deep sense of alienation for many Sox fans. One of the centerpieces for this trade was shortstop Mike Caruso. Sox management hoped the young shortstop would prove the trade worthwhile. Caruso actually hit .306 in 1998 but had the power of a wet noodle. But with the score tied at four in the eighth in game three, Caruso sent a two-run home run into the basket in right field to put the Sox ahead 6-4. The score held up and the underdog Sox had their sweep.

Rob Sweas of West Chicago attended the game with his father. Because of another rain delay, many fans left, Sweas says he dodged some 80-year-old Wrigley ushers and found himself in prime box seats by the Sox dugout. He said Sox fans went berserk after the Caurso home run that would have been an out in many other stadiums, Cub fans "slouched in their chairs, realizing what ridicule they would have to take. After we left the park," Sweas says, "my dad and I waved a broom through the sun roof of our car, beeping our horn and driving through the streets around Wrigleyville."

After this series, the Cub season went bye-bye. The Sox only ended up with 75 wins, (though that was more than the Cubs) but showed some real spark and went on to win the division the next year. Meanwhile the Cubs saw their team disintegrate with a string of embarrassing defeats, ending their streak of post-season appearances at one. But for Sox fans like Sweas, the June sweep in the Cubs cute little ballpark helped keep them warm in what normally would have been a cold off-season.

Triumphant Return
Could these guys be for real?

At first glance, the June 19, 2000 Sox home game against the Cleveland Indians looked like just another game on the schedule. This game became more important because Chicago was in first place, and the Indians were their closest pursuer. What was really important, however, was the reception the Sox had received upon return from a rather successful road trip.

It is not hard for any Chicago baseball fan to be skeptical of their team being in first place in June. It has all happened before and the inevitable fall usually followed. In June 2000, however, the Chicago White Sox began to show their fans that they a little different.

On the preceding road trip, just after beating the Cubs two out of three, Chicago played three games against the Indians and four against New York. From 1995 to 1999, these two teams represented the American League in the World Series. Winning on the road is never easy, and observers thought three or four victories would help the Sox establish credibility with their fans.

Chicago won all seven, scoring 65 runs in the process. In the last game, the White Sox made the defending World Champion Yankees look like little leaguers scoring nine in the first inning en route to a 17-4 stomping. New Yorkers, never known for their sensitivity, were duly impressed with the Sox and laced their own team with boos and derision.

Although the Sox are a team with a chronic attendance problem, attendance was not a problem on that June 19 evening after the Sox returned home from that road trip. Matt Cianchetti had tickets for the game. He wanted to see his favorite team solidify its hold on first and couldn't resist going to the game after the team's 7-0 trip through Cleveland and New York.

"I went online on the Sunday night before the game and purchased two tickets which to my surprise were all the way in the 500 level of the upper deck," Cianchetti wrote to the author. "As most Sox fans know this was unheard of for our team to be this close to a sellout on a weekday night. We knew it was going to be a huge jacked up crowd and that we would have to leave early. We ended up leaving early but getting snarled in a standstill traffic jam on the Kennedy Expressway anyway. The source for this huge traffic jam? The Thirty-First and Thirty-Fifth Street exits to Comiskey Park! It had traffic backed up all the way through the Loop.

"By the time we got to the ball park exits, it was already in the fourth inning and we were listening to Ed Farmer and John Rooney [Sox radio announcers] call the game as the Sox were laying another whipping on second place Cleveland. All of the parking lots were sold out, and there were thousands milling about the ballpark looking for tickets. At this point, we decided to cut our losses on the Upper Deck tickets and call it a night. We took the rest of the game in at a local bar.

"We later heard on the radio that the game was a complete sellout and the reason all the parking lots sold out was because an estimated Fifty-six thousand people descended on the ballpark. Maybe they just thought they could just park and go up to the window and buy tickets only to find out the game was sold out completely. Not to mention they blocked those who had tickets from getting in."

The Sox won 6-1 behind the pitching of Kip Wells, and Cianchetti never got closer to the game than a TV set. He wasn't overly disappointed.

"Even though I was disappointed we couldn't make it to the ballpark, I was happy that White Sox fever was gripping Chicago," Cianchetti wrote. "It was the most unforgettable game I never made it to."

Early Wynn delivers the first pitch of 1959 World Series. Wynn threw seven shutout innings in an 11-0 thrashing of the Dodgers. It was the most lopsided post-season win in franchise history. Sox fans dreamed of a sweep; they were a little disappointed. (Gerry Bilek photo collection.)

The typical way the "Go-Go White Sox" earned a run, catcher Sherman Lollar hits into a double play while Nelson Fox scores. The run gave Chicago a 1-0 win in Game Five of the 1959 World Series, but it was much too little, much too late. (Courtesy of the Mark Fletcher Photo Collection.)

Nelson Fox congratulates pitcher Dick Donovan after Donovan saved the Game Five 1-0 win. 92,706 fans witnessed the yet-still last White Sox World Series win. (Courtesy of the Leo Bauby Photo Collection.)

Having hit another World Series homer, Ted Kluszewski is greeted at home plate by Al Smith (No. 16), Jim Landis (No. 1), and Sherman Lollar (No. 10). Kluszewski had hit his third homer of the series and collected RBIs 8, 9, and 10. His 10 RBIs is still a record for a six game World Series, a mark he shares with Hall of Famer Yogi Berra. The homer gave the Sox some life in Game Six, but the Dodgers won 9-3 to take the series four games to two. (Courtesy of the Gerry Bilek Collection.)

A Bat Day at Old Comiskey Park on an undisclosed date. It was one promotion that always turned out right. The Bat Day on May 20, 1973, produced the largest crowd ever at Comiskey, attracting 55,555 fans. It is possible that nearly 60,000 people showed at Old Comiskey that day. (Courtesy of the Mark Fletcher Photo Collection.)

Disco records meet their doom on July 12, 1979, between games of a doubleheader against the Tigers. The exploding scoreboard couldn't have done a better job. (Courtesy of the Gerry Bilek Photo Collection.)

They say a picture paints a thousand words, but this picture doesn't show the worst or the extent of an event, Disco Demolition, that was one of the biggest embarrassments of the franchise—other that not winning a World Series in 86 years, that is. (Courtesy of the Gerry Bilek Photo Collection.)

No, this damage was not caused by Disco Demolition. Old Comiskey had some serious drainage problems after a rock concert in 1979. (Courtesy of the Leo Bauby Photo Collection.)

Martians invade Old Comiskey in 1959. They were friendly, but shortstop Luis Aparicio doesn't look amused. (Courtesy of the Mark Fletcher Photo Collection.)

White Sox players meet on the field after the last Old Comiskey game. Just imagine a Greg Luzinksi homer banging off one of the light towers or a Dick Allen clout clearing that tall center field wall. Many people were teary eyed that day. (Photo by Mark Fletcher.)

Here is the outfield view of last game played at Comiskey Park on September 30, 1990. The message on the scoreboard lists the attendance for the year, which was 2,002,359. (Photo by Gerry Bilek.)

A special moment, as the scoreboard erupts for the last time. The Sox had just finished playing their last night game at Old Comiskey. The time on the scoreboard clock freezes

114

the moment. The image shows a stately stadium that will never be forgotten. (Photo by James A. Rasmussen.)

Just another aftermath to another save by Bobby Thigpen in 1990, his 57th. His single season save record of that year still stands today. But it just wasn't any save. His ninth inning work preserved a 2-1 win over the Seattle Mariners. The win just made the last game at Old Comiskey more emotional. (Photo by Mark Fletcher.)

Nancy Faust says good-bye to Old Comiskey. The organist has been a large part of the White Sox since she began entertaining fans in 1970. Faust originated the "Hey, hey, Good-bye" song that Sox fans love and opponents hate. September 30, 1990 was an emotional day for the popular Faust who still is at her station at the organ today. (Photo by Gerry Bilek Photo.)

Old Comiskey is captured in one of its stages of destruction. (Photo by Mark Fletcher.)

Cubs Manager Leo Durocher and White Sox skipper Eddie Stanky look friendly enough in 1967. Back then Sox-Cubs games didn't count. Stanky had actually played for Durocher and the two formed a mutual admiration society. (Courtesy of the Gerry Bilek Photo Collection)

EIGHT

Other Great Moments

There really are too many great moments to recall.

Those rooftop homers: A shot onto or over the Old Comiskey Park roof was not something that happened very often. Only 13 White Sox players did it on a total of 22 occasions. One of the most talked about homers was Dave Nicholson's drive estimated at 573 feet on May 6, 1964. There is a controversy about whether the homer actually hit the back end of the roof before exiting the stadium. Buddy Bradford hit one on April 25, 1969, proving that he didn't need the pulled in fences that Arthur Allyn had erected to reduce Comiskey's dimensions. Tom Egan was the next to hit one on July 25, 1971. Egan hit 10 homers in only 251 official at-bats that year.

There couldn't be a list of such slugging without Dick Allen. Allen blasted one off Mike Cuellar on May 1, 1973. Of course the list also wouldn't be complete without a member of the South Side Hit Men. Richie Zisk launched one on June 4, 1977 against Don Gullet.

Then there was the tag team of Greg Luzinksi and Ron Kittle who accomplished this a total of 11 times between them, five coming in the Winning Ugly 1983 season. Ten of those homers were hit when the plate was moved eight feet closer to the outfield. On August 1, 1984, Carlton Fisk hit one on the roof following one of Kittle's other roof shots that day.

Unfortunately, not many great things happened to the roof top sluggers after their feats. Dave Nicholson didn't hit anything when he wasn't hitting homers and never had much of a career. Buddy Bradford looked like he could be a real power hitter, but could never be consistent and his outfield play drove fans crazy. Tom Egan had a short career. Greg Luzinksi was out of baseball just two years after his big roof top year. Ron Kittle never matched his power numbers after his rookie season. But those homers were something to see.

Those pitching performances: Wilbur Wood won two consecutive games on the same day. This was amazing even for Wood. He pitched five innings in the relief win of a suspended game started on May 26, after 16 innings, and resumed on May 28. After pitching those five innings to pick up the win, Wood went out and started the regularly schedule contest. He then pitched a complete game shut out, giving up only four hits. All in all he logged in 14 innings, giving up one run and six hits, earning his 12th and 13th wins. That is right: 13 wins before the kids got out of school.

Joe Cowley pitched no-hitter, September 19, 1986. It is hard to say a no-hitter isn't a pretty thing, but Cowley struggled with his control in this game. He walked seven, which led to a seventh inning run for the Angels at Anaheim. But a no-hitter is a no-hitter, and it beat a game he pitched on May 28 of that year when he struck out the first seven Rangers he faced only to lose when he couldn't get past the fifth inning.

Those historic games: Harold Baines ended a 25-inning, two-day game against the Brewers with a center field homer. On May 9, 1984, Baines won the game with a 400-foot plus shot off Milwaukee's Chuck Porter. The eight hour and six minute game stands as the longest in American League history. Baines' homer was just another one of his clutch hits.

And who could forget the "Brawl Game" against the Detroit Tigers April 22, 2000. The White Sox were off to a good start in 2000 and used the Tiger pitching staff for batting practice that sunny spring afternoon in Chicago. By the end of six, Chicago led 10-1. Tiger starter Jeff Weaver hit Paul Konerko in the fourth and Carlos Lee in the sixth. Sox lefty Jim Parque responded by plunking Dean Palmer in the seventh. Palmer rushed the mound and it was a free for all. The bean balls weren't over with. In the ninth Sox reliever Bobby Howry hit Shane Halter. The benches emptied again. All in all, 11 players were ejected.

The game itself? The Sox won 14-6. They took the Central division. The Tigers finished in third nowhere near the lead and sank to last in 2003 with a worse record than the 1970 Sox.

Luis Aparicio, arguably was the best defensive shortstop in the history of the White Sox, catches a pop up at the 1962 All-Star Game, July 10, 1962. He had two stints with the White Sox and stole 56 bases during the 1959 pennant-winning season. Notice the halo on the hat of Los Angeles Angel Billy Moran. (Courtesy of the Gerry Bilek Photo Collection.)

Nelson Fox reaches another milestone, becoming the 40th major league player to pick up 2,500 hits, on July 28, 1963. The hit was off Baltimore lefty Dave McNally in a game the Sox won 4-1. Fox was one of the most popular players in White Sox history. At one time he played in 798 consecutive games. His last .300 season was in the pennant-winning season of 1959 when he hit .306 and was named American League Most Valuable Player. (Courtesy of the Gerry Bilek Photo Collection.)

Dave Nicholson, a guy that could hit the ball a long way when he made contact, just couldn't couldn't make contact enough. He hit a 573 foot homer on May 6, 1964, at Old Comiskey, but was coming off a 1963 season when he struck out 175 times. He never became the slugger the Sox so desperately needed. (Courtesy of the Mark Fletcher Photo Collection,)

Dave Nicholson is seen here after hitting one of his two grand slams in 1963. (Courtesy of the Leo Bauby Photo Collection.)

One of the most popular White
Sox players in the '60s, Ken Berry
is unable to come up with long
fly off the bat of Twins shortstop
Zoillo Versailles in a 1965 game at
Comiskey. Berry played center field
with abandon, one time throwing
his whole body over the short
center field fence in pursuit of a
home run. The White Sox won this
game 2-1. (Courtesy of the Gerry
Bilek Photo Collection)

Roland Hemond, one of the most
popular White Sox front office
men. He helped revive the franchise
during the early '70s. (Courtesy of
Roland Hemond.)

123

Greg Luzinski holds three balls signifying his three roof shots in 1983. Luzinski hit 32 homers that year and was an imposing figure in the middle of the lineup, especially during the last half of the season. He also hit a mammoth home run in a key win over the Royals in Kansas City on August 22. But his '83 post season wasn't so hot. (Courtesy of the Mark Fletcher Photo Collection.)

Francisco Barrios delivers from the mound at Comiskey Park. Barrios had a load of potential when he came up to the White Sox in 1976, and was part of a two-man no-hitter that year and won 14 in 1977. Tragically, his potential went unfulfilled, and his life ended way too soon. (Courtesy of the Leo Bauby Photo Collection.)

A young Robin Ventura is seen here in the early stages of his career. Ventura, one the best third baseman in White Sox history, hit a dramatic home run off Dennis Eckersley in the later stages of the 1993 pennant race. On September 19, 1993, the White Sox were in a close pennant race, only $3\frac{1}{2}$ ahead of the Rangers. In a tough game against Oakland, the Sox faced Dennis Eckersley in a 1-1 tie in the ninth at Oakland. Eckersley was Mr. Automatic back then, many times setting the side down in order to earn a save or keeping his team in a game during a save type assignment. Frank Thomas, who had been 0 for 8 lifetime against Eckersley, singled. Ventura, 0 for 6 against Eck, clobbered a home run over the right center field wall. The Sox won 3-1, gained a game on Texas and never looked back, clinching their second Western Division title eight days later. Ventura and Frank Thomas would give the Sox a strong sense of identity during the '90s. (Photo by Mark Fletcher.)

Tom Paciorek sliding into second base during the longest time-wise game in major league baseball history. The contest took eight hours and six minutes to complete over two days with the Sox beating the Milwaukee Brewers 7-6 in 25 innings on a Harold Baines homer. The May 9-10, 1984 game was one of the few highlights of that disappointing season. Paciorek eventually worked as a color TV man for the Sox. (Courtesy of the Mark Fletcher Photo Collection.)

Sox pitcher Joe Cowley is in high kicking action. He won 11 for the Sox in 1986 and threw an ugly looking no-hitter. (Courtesy of the Leo Bauby Photo Collection.)

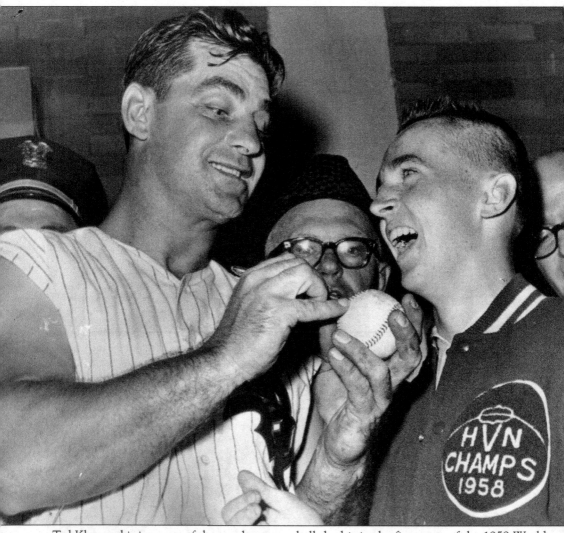

Ted Kluszewski signs one of the two home run balls he hit in the first game of the 1959 World Series. Fan Mike Cummings looks on with glee. Norman Rockwell couldn't have painted a better picture. (Courtesy of the Gerry Bilek Photo Collection.)

Visit us at
arcadiapublishing.com

CPSIA information can be obtained
at www.ICGtesting.com
Printed in the USA
LVOW04*1008120717

541102LV00014B/95/P

9 781531 618650